INTRODUCT

Just how lucky can one person get? It's an interesting question and I think that I would qualify easily for being on the podium in terms of good fortune. How about this? When I was 16 years old I used to dream, quite literally fantasise, about owning a pair of gloves because I got very uncomfortable riding my 250 BSA in the wet and cold of what was a very early autumn that year. It wasn't much of an aspiration but it was about as much as a kid from the wrong side of town, with no prospects, could manage.

As for a fantasy bike, I couldn't have even created a wish list because it would have been so far removed from my world. I would have liked both brakes on my BSA to work, or the headlamp to come on when it was dark, but mainly I wanted to ride any motorcycle I could lay my hands on – all day, every day, from the moment I got up until I fell into bed at night – because, truly, I was the hardest of hard core addicts where motorcycles and motorcycling were concerned

I never had much in the way of ability as a rider but I did have two invaluable talents. First, I found that I could ride anything with two wheels instantly and competently. Never with any great flair or ability but certainly without any fuss, training or advice. Give me a bike and I could make it work.

I also discovered that I had a real aptitude for being able to put my passion for motorcycling into words and so magazines were happy to pay me to write stories for them and, very fortunately for me, readers liked them too.

So, at 16 I was painting shelves in an engineering merchant's store and four years later I was having lunch with the managing director of BSA and being treated as a minor VIP. You can read this surprising story in the first part of my autobiography, A Penguin in a Sparrow's Nest – www.frankmelling.com

The dream continues to this day. I have been incredibly blessed in being allowed to ride bikes which only a privileged few have ever thrown a leg over – you won't find that many people who have ridden a Moto Guzzi V8 Grand Prix racer – and I have been equally lucky to take part in a vast range of motorcycling activities.

But I still know my place in the world. I'm just a very ordinary rider who, by some miraculous quirks of fate, has done extraordinary things with motorcycles.

I hope that you enjoy joining me on what has truly been The Ride of My Life... because it's been fantastic fun.

With very best wishes

Frank Melling

Author and concept: Frank Melling

Editor and photography: Carol Melling

Production editors: Sarah Wilkinson, Tim Hartley

Design: Kelvin Clements, Michael Baumber

Publisher: Steve O'Hara

Publishing director: Dan Savage

Commercial director: Nigel Hole

Printed by: William Gibbons And Sons, Wolverhampton

ISBN: 978-1-911276-55-5

Published by: Mortons Media Group Ltd, Media Centre, Morton Way, Horncastle, Lincolnshire, LN9 6JR Tel: 01507 529529

© 2017 Mortons Media Group Ltd. .

MORTONS
MEDIA GROUP LTD

CONTENTS

THANKS

The world of motorcycling is a wonderful place to work and is full of hyper-enthusiastic people who are also very kind. Thanks to their support I have been able to ride virtually every type of powered two-wheeler ever made.

Some of these enthusiasts – and they really all do love bikes – come from inside the motorcycle industry. In particular, I owe a great debt to Sammy Miller who has let me ride some of his museum's most exotic bikes. Sammy has one of the great museums in the world. You can find out all about it from www.sammymiller.co.uk

The National Motorcycle Museum – www.nationalmotorcyclemuseum.co.uk – houses the world's greatest collection of British bikes and I have been incredibly fortunate to be able to ride some of its rarest bikes too.

Lawrence Rose, of Classic Motorcycles Ltd – classicbritishbikes. ebaymp.co.uk – kindly lets me borrow a lot of bikes from his huge stock of immaculate machines.

Ben Walker, at Bonhams, also generously loaned machines from the stunning collections of bikes he auctions.

Legendary motorcycle industry icons, like Triumph's Norman Hyde and Les Williams and the staff of the Moto Guzzi museum in Mandello del Lario, have been unstintingly generous in sharing their knowledge with me.

Finally, a huge thanks to all private owners who have trusted me with their precious machines.

As I often say, writing about the motorcycles I love is vastly better than having a real job!

I also want to give a particular thanks to Knox – www.planet-knox.com – which makes much of the life protecting body armour and clothing I rely on. My relationship with Knox is a slightly odd, and very lively, one. If I don't like a Knox product – or an idea – then I will tell Geoff, Margaret and Jennifer unequivocally – and they don't get all angry and hormonal as do many companies. We just agree to disagree.

But the truth, the absolute truth, is that I believe the Knox products I use are the best in their category.

For example, I wear a range of Knox back protectors not because I am given them free of charge but because I know that there is nothing better. The same equipment protects Carol.

I also respect the integrity of the company and I admire hugely the fact that all Knox equipment is designed in Britain and that a lot of it is made in Cockermouth, up on the wild and beautiful Cumbrian coast.

So, for all these reasons, when we were looking for a commercial partner Knox was the first, and only, choice. Knox's financial support has helped us to produce a coffee table quality book at the price of a magazine.

Producing a book is very much a team effort in which the person writing the words has a surprisingly small, and insignificant, part to play. I have been incredibly lucky to have a great team at Mortons to work with on this project. Encouraged by Steve, Dan blessed the whole project and it was launched with all of Mortons' considerable resources behind it.

Kelvin and Mike then had to put up with me harassing them to death to get the designs to the outstanding level they are – and that wasn't a two minute job!

Sarah and Tim then shepherded *Ride of My Life* to completion – and that wasn't a straightforward job either!

Assisting wherever they could were a lot of other people – Jane, Charlie and Mortons' editorial, show and advertising staff.

A genuine, heartfelt, thanks to everyone for helping us make *Ride of My Life* the best we could achieve.

However, the book wouldn't have been possible without Carol, the Swiss Army Knife of wives. Virtually all of the images in the book come from Carol's skill with a camera, and her meticulous and insightful editing has made the best of what writing skills I have.

But, most importantly, Carol smiles when I am fed up, snarls at me when I wander off target and holds my hand, literally and metaphorically, every time I work with her.

She's also a brilliant race mechanic and, fortunately for me, she says that she isn't available to anyone else, which is a real relief!

For BSA fans, the
Rocket 3 is still a
true thoroughbred

BSA ROCKET 3

A TRIPLE TRAGEDY

I wrote this story at an interesting time in world history and one which got me thinking about issues bigger than bikes... and there actually are some!

At the time, President Trump was becoming increasingly worried about the threat from North Korean nuclear armed intercontinental missiles which were almost – but not quite – able to reach the west coast of the USA. He was also teetering on the edge of war with Russia having attacked a Syrian airbase. The world was becoming an increasingly dangerous place for us all.

I hope that things have calmed down by the time you read this story because riding motorcycles is infinitely more fun, and a much nicer thing to do than killing people: it really is. »

For future historians, assuming that there is any interest in British bikes 50 years from now, the most transparent window on to the reasons for the death of the British motorcycle industry might well be the BSA/Triumph triples – a tragedy which would have made Shakespeare proud.

Currently, the three cylinder machines have a fanatical following and their acolytes will hear no wrong of them. However, this is what Bert Hopwood, BSA's group engineering director, thought of the model in 1981.

"The triple machine which found its way to market in 1968 was a flop, and it was not until we reverted to the original prototype style that it started to sell and earn revenue. It (the BSA/Triumph triple) should have been in production in 1963, thus five years of production were lost, the Japanese became ever more firmly entrenched and our reputation suffered yet another severe setback."

So what went wrong (and right too)? – for this very simple machine did achieve some outstanding results.

The 'wrong' element is multi-layered but is centred round weak senior management and political in-fighting which made the Roman court of Caligula look like a play school Christmas party.

Let's start at the very beginning. The oft quoted myth is that Bert Hopwood and Doug Hele, Triumph's chief development engineer, were like father and son. This is wrong in fact. I came to know Doug reasonably well and I was the last person to interview him, just a few days before his death. Hele's view of Hopwood was unambivalent: he neither liked nor respected him.

This is how Hele described the much vaunted BSA MC1 which Hopwood had designed as a world beating racer: "It had a quite serious set-back, in so far as the valves were the wrong way round and so would not open. The radial valves couldn't work because they got entangled. But it was very stylish…

"The bike wouldn't have handled either. The original frame was very much like a 7R and simply would not have worked in a racing environment. Other than that, it was very stylish."

In 1962, Hele had been headhunted from Norton by Hopwood. Doug jumped at the opportunity because Norton had been taken over by AMC and was becoming very much the junior partner in the enlarged company.

Hopwood, to his credit, saw the end of the road for the 650cc twins. In particular, he disliked the harshness of the larger Triumph twins as ever more power was squeezed out of them. The problem was that the twins were the children of the autocratic Edward Turner whose word was law at Triumph – and within the wider BSA Group too. Senior management's adoration of Turner was to be a major issue in the triple tragedy.

Hele, an enthusiastic advocate for three cylinder engines, felt that the only solution was to add another cylinder to the 500cc Triumph twin and provide a stop-gap triple until the planned ohc engines came on stream.

Turner famously thought the idea "potty" – not for any engineering reasons but simply because the new engine was not a twin but a triple.

Regardless, Hopwood recalls the moment that the triple egg was actually fertilised.

"One evening, late in 1963, after everyone had gone home, we sat in his (Hele's) office and to amuse ourselves we laid out the basic outline of what later became the 750cc, three-cylinder Trident.

"We thought that the result was very encouraging indeed, but in view of the rather abortive conversation which I had already had with the managing director (Edward Turner), this drawing was filed away as a memento."

In fact, this is not what happened. Doug had a drawing board in his front room at home and there, in his own time, he drew the triple engine – and, in view of the constraints he was working under, he was very proud of the design.

This is Hele again: "He (Hopwood) was also keen to claim credit wherever possible. The Triumph T150 triple was entirely my design regardless of what Hopwood, or anyone else, said later. I drew the Triumph triple completely unaided and on my own."

Doug had the complete engine drawings finished by early 1964. It's worth remembering »

BSA version of the triple engine, with its 15° of forward lean, looks vastly better than the vertical Triumph version

that this was a full five years before Honda's 750 four-cylinder machine and even a year before the Japanese factory's launch of the CB450 twin.

This point needs stressing. Triumph could have been selling its 750cc triple when the biggest, and fastest, Japanese four-stroke opposition came from the 450cc Honda.

The BSA Group stood in front of an open goal, with the ball ready to kick and the opposition team not even in the stadium – but only if they concentrated a lot of effort on the bike.

Much as I admire Hele, and my admiration – and affection – for this wonderful engineer is truly unbounded, Doug was not a great designer. A more apposite description would be to say that he was the world's best garden shed designer and the triple reflects this. As a piece of practical, cost saving engineering using the minimum of new tooling, the engine is a work of genius. Critically, it could have been garden shed cheap, as well as garden shed simple, to put into production.

Not that the first version of the triple engine

was fit for purpose, because it wasn't. Norman Hyde was an apprentice in the Triumph experimental department and remembers that Hele's first version of the triple was full of faults.

"There were problems with the oil pump which was of shaft drive design. The iron barrels were also a real issue and caused the cylinder head to leak.

"But the biggest issue was with the gear primary drive. The coefficient of expansion of aluminium, and the distance between the crankshaft and the clutch, meant that the gear drive was never going to be successful – and it wasn't!

"The bore and stroke of the engine was altered from the original 63mm x 80mm, which was the configuration of the pre-unit Speedtwin, to 67mm x 70mm, as used on the unit construction singles."

Despite the engine not being ready for production, Hele took the finished design into Meriden and there were two reactions. First, Hopwood took over the project and claimed

Rocket 3 has a lot of road presence even today

"IF THE RIVALRY BETWEEN MERIDEN AND SMALL HEATH WAS FIERCE IN ENGLAND, IT WAS NEAR PSYCHOPATHIC IN THE US..."

credit for it. Secondly, it immediately became mired in BSA Group politics.

With the nominal retirement of Edward Turner, although he did remain as a non-executive director of the BSA Group and his looming spectre still walked the corridors of power both at Small Heath and Meriden, McKinsey & Co–an American management consultancy firm–was brought in, to completely re-vamp the company.

Harry Sturgeon was appointed group managing director. He came from The Churchill Grinding Machine Company, another BSA company, but knew nothing about motorcycles.

The politics are important to the practical parts of the triple's story because all the BSA group senior management had bigger fish to fry than Doug's garden shed special. Harry Sturgeon was obsessive about increasing production and, from an outsider's point of view, Triumph was selling everything it could make, so what could possibly be wrong?

As McKinsey tried to build a single, highly centralised motorcycle manufacturing entity within the BSA Group, so infighting and the desire to protect individual empires became ever more frenetic.

One triple prototype, the P1, was made and, in a wonderfully ironic reprise of Turner's shoe horning of his Speedtwin engine into the chassis of Triumph's single cylinder Tiger 90, Hele squeezed the new three cylinder engine into a Bonneville frame. And what a lovely thing it was too–very Bonnevilleish and yet clearly different.

There were initial problems with the width of the engine, and the cylinder head gasket sealing, but these were quickly resolved and the bike was ready for production in the Autumn of 1965–ready for the following year's critical spring selling season in the USA.

Norman Hyde again: "The bike had flaws but we had skilled fitters who were capable of looking at fits and suggesting solutions to management. I was an apprentice but even I was involved in the discussions. Bert Hopwood would come down and say to me: "Well young Hyde, what do you think of this?"

So what stopped the triple going into production? First, and most importantly, the

reorganisation of the BSA Group motorcycle manufacturing in an attempt to unify it. The demotion, or early retirement, of key managers also actively helped build the disaster.

Ariel was closed and the already tense relations between BSA and Triumph reached new heights. It was said, with a degree of justification, that Triumph would rather share its research with Honda than BSA–and, to be fair, vice-versa was equally true!

Then there was a chaotic dilution of effort. Hopwood wanted a modular family of singles, twins and triples and these were to be based around an 83cc single which would morph into a 249cc triple. There was to be an eight speed, dohc, GP racer and a six-speed sohc road bike. All this was wonderful–but nothing happened. Meanwhile, the eminently production-ready triple prototype remained at the back of the queue.

Turner also had his hand in the pie and, in semi-retirement, had designed the disastrous BSA Bandit/Triumph Fury triple which suffered from a multitude of engineering problems.

It's worth recording just how bad this engine was. Here is an extract from Hopwood's report about the bike to the BSA Main Board:

"The complete motorcycle (BSA Bandit/Triumph Fury) we have on test now has 5400 miles registered and in this mileage 3000 have been completed by a tester who rode most of the time at very low speeds because of the severe problems.

"The machine used four pints of oil every 100 miles and the tests are worthless because of a lack of power. The other 2400 miles by various riders embraced four complete rebuilds of the engine unit due to failures of the crankshaft, gudgeon pins and main bearings.

"The frame of the machine has already been redesigned due to excess flexibility in the main, which constituted a hazard and the front forks are also considered to be fundamentally unsafe."

Another shambles was taking place at Small Heath and this was a very different elephant squeezing into the group's already overcrowded R&D bathroom.

Jeff Smith had won the 1964 and 1965 World 500cc Motocross Championships, and the »

BSA-ists were determined to get a third world title – if only to put their sworn enemies at Meriden in their place!

BSA competition manager Brian Martin's idea was to build the lightest 500cc motocross bike in the world. It was to have an all titanium frame and the engine was largely magnesium and titanium. In terms of engineering, this was at the far end of cutting edge – and it was a disaster.

On paper, the bike was a world beater. Four-stroke pulling power and traction with the weight of a two-stroke should have swept all before it, but things went disastrously wrong right from the start and the Ti bike was soon scrapped.

Not only did the Ti BSA consume a huge amount of money and engineering time but there was another, unreported problem. Before his untimely death I was very close friends with Fred Barlow who, as an apprentice, worked on the Ti project. Fred and I spent many happy hours discussing the tales of the numerous 'foreigners' which were done by BSA tool room staff to help the race team. These unofficial jobs caused BSA works manager Al Cave to call the race shop staff: "The worst of professional thieves…" because they not only stole materials but vital, and irreplaceable, tool room time and staff from production R&D effort.

Could things get worse? Well, yes they could – and considerably so too. At the time, the distribution for the BSA Group products was chaotic. Triumph Baltimore and Triumph Los Angeles handled Meriden products while east coast BSA sales were in the hands of BSA New Jersey, and in the west by the privately owned Hap Alzina Company based in Oakland, California.

If the rivalry between Meriden and Small Heath was fierce in England, it was near psychopathic in the US with each organisation running its own race teams and often battling it out for publicity with their sister company. It would have never happened in Japan.

Rocket 3 instrumentation was a real parts bin special when the bike really deserved something better

The realpolitik of the situation was that any new BSA Group product which looked like a money spinner had to be given, in fair shares, to both BSA and Triumph dealers. This I feel, more than any other factor, was the reason for the two different versions of the triple.

Meanwhile, in this maelstrom of political infighting and management ineptitude, Hele's garden shed special took a back seat, which was a real shame because the bike worked a treat. Now acceptably slim after some further Hele tweaking, the engine produced a reliable and consistent 58hp at 7250rpm – against 45ish from a Bonneville – and was smooth and torquey. Almost as important, just like Turner's Speedtwin, the emotional gap from the old bike to the new one was narrow because the new triple felt very Triumphy.

Again like a Speedtwin, the weight was perfect being only 40lb heavier than a Bonnie. Now, Triumph owners could have a much faster, smoother and sexier bike but one which didn't alienate them: perfect in every way for the 1965 season.

But no. That would have been too sensible.

The crunch came when Harry Sturgeon, who had been very ill with a brain tumour, announced the news that Honda was about to release a 750cc four cylinder bike. Now this really was a gigantic tank parked on the BSA Group's lawn and the board went into full panic mode in an attempt to give their dealers something with which they could compete. In actual fact, it wasn't going to be a something but two somethings – to keep American dealers sweet.

At this point in the story, it would be easy to criticise Ogle Design and the mess it made

"ANOTHER SHAMBLES WAS TAKING PLACE AT SMALL HEATH AND THIS WAS A VERY DIFFERENT ELEPHANT SQUEEZING INTO THE GROUP'S ALREADY OVERCROWDED R&D BATHROOM."

The eight inch, twin leading shoe drum brake borrowed from Triumph's Bonneville works well but should really have been a disc

When the Rocket 3 was launched, BSA's teenage fans actively and enthusiastically loathed the 'ray gun' silencers

Rocket 3 manual choke and kick starting were pure 1950s

of the triple's styling. Certainly, at the time, I was right at the front of the loathing queue. As a 16 year old, I knew what a British sports bike should look like and it was predicated on being sleek and feline – with an undisguised eagerness to go fast.

Now, with the benefit of long sight, and maybe even a tiny smidgen of wisdom, I can see what happened. In 1967, anything was possible – as long as it was 'modern' – and with a capital 'M'. You could walk past a tip and see magnificent Victorian mahogany sideboards piled up for firewood simply for being old fashioned. I had, very briefly before she dumped me for being far beneath her social standing, a girlfriend whose proudest possession was a piece of plastic on a pink, Terylene cord which her brother had brought back from swinging Carnaby Street. Modern was good – and everything else was bad.

Ogle Design had already styled the Raleigh Chopper bicycle – a truly dreadful thing – and was now given the task of making the triples properly space age.

The problem was that the brief from BSA was vague and confusing.

Jim English, from Ogle, remembers the

shambles: "We were told they (BSA) wanted a flashy American look, like a Cadillac. We really let our hair down doing futuristic stuff. I never thought that BSA would go for my flared silencer with three tail pipes. To be honest, as a motorcyclist, I thought that the Triumph they brought in (the P2 prototype) looked fine just as it was."

So, instead of the lithe, slim, sporty and eager 120mph sports bike we all wanted, Ogle gave us a dumpy, square machine borrowed from a Flash Gordon comic strip – and we enthusiastically reviled it.

Most of all we hated the 'ray gun' silencers which gave the bike a big fat bum – and, in the interests of political correctness, I'll not explore this area further!

If the styling was a mess, the specification wasn't much better. At this point, let me reiterate the launch date: 1968. If the bike had been on sale three years earlier, things would have been very different.

The problems began the moment a triple was wheeled out of the garage because the engines needed kicking into life: no electric boot here. The starting procedure was straight from the 1950s motorcyclists' handbook. 'Tickle' »

"...WE HATED THE 'RAY GUN' SILENCERS WHICH GAVE THE BIKE A BIG FAT BUM—AND, IN THE INTERESTS OF POLITICAL CORRECTNESS, I'LL NOT EXPLORE THIS AREA FURTHER!"

the outside of the two Amal carburettors – a wonderfully sanitised verb which meant that you held the float chamber down until petrol slobbered all over your gloves and on to the engine.

Then, set the cable operated choke at ¼, ½ or ¾ position according to the ambient temperature and swing the long kick starter until the engine coughed into life. In 1958, this was acceptable. Ten years later it wasn't.

The triples were four-speeders which was inexcusable. Six-speed gearboxes were very well proven in racing. From the late 1950s they could be bought over the counter, from Austrian Michael Schafleitner, by anyone with a healthy bank account. In 1965, Quaife Engineering in England began making five-speed clusters and these were used by Triumph for racing.

An ultra-modern, space age, flagship product absolutely demanded a five-speed gearbox. Meriden actually had the five-speed Quaife gearbox available. That this wasn't put into the Rocket 3 was unforgiveable!

BSA also knew about disc brakes. It had used an Airheart disc on the ill-fated Ti motocross machine and its West Coast office was well aware of the Lockhart discs. Instead, the Competition Department chose to use the twin leading shoe front brake from the existing Bonneville range.

Despite anything Ogle tried do with the styling, kick-starting a four-speed gearbox and the bike's drum brakes made the triple old fashioned at launch.

Of the two bikes, my teenage loyalty drifted towards BSA. I knew that one day, when I was a big boy, I was going to grow up and race motocross and be a world champion on a BSA and lots of pretty girls wearing little, tiny, fluorescent yellow mini-skirts and circle stitched bras would sit in the front of my van and share my bag of chips and look admiringly, and hopefully longingly too, at the big trophy on the dashboard – and maybe even a little bit at me as well. Incredibly, a few bits of the fantasy actually happened so you never know your luck in life's raffle…

The BSA 'Flamboyant Red' was nicer than Triumph's green and the 15° inclination on

the cylinders also looked sportier than the Trident's upright cylinders. Finally, the BSA duplex frame was much racier. Given an alloy tank, a pair of clip ons, some rear sets and long tapered meggas, my 16-year-old brain could see me riding a Rocket 3.

The problem was that, like all garden shed specials, the engine was a nightmare to mass produce. The two-valve, push-rod operated engine was superficially simple, and old fashioned, but the asymmetric, vertically split crankcases were a cheap solution to expensive tooling.

As for an electric starter, this was absolutely necessary – but only the Japanese would provide it for you.

Disregarding Ogle's lumpen styling, the rest of the cycle parts were actually rather nice. The Rocket 3 duplex frame was a typical BSA product and provided excellent handling. Interestingly, Norman Hyde – a Triumph man to the core – doesn't like it. Truly, plus ça change plus c'est la même chose!

Hele was very familiar with both the Oldani and Fontana race brakes and you can see the Italian manufacturers' influence in the rough cast, 8in (200mm) twin leading shoe front brake from the 1968 Bonneville which is really rather good. Certainly, this race derived stopper is light years better than the die cast, conical brake which replaced it. The 7in (180mm) rear brake, although dating from the 1950s, works okay.

The narrow front mudguard is really neat, and enthusiasm for the '3' starts to build – until you reach the crude Smiths speedometer and tachometer which, accompanied by agricultural switch gear and wiring, takes you straight back to the 1950s.

So what did you get for your £895? The first thing was a real shock. In 1966, the average annual wage – what a skilled tradesman would be earning – was £891, so it was going to take a whole year to buy a triple.

Then you got what was effectively a Bonneville with an extra cylinder and with styling you didn't like.

Finally, quality control was extremely variable, so you could expect to be taking your

For its day, the Rocket 3 was a big lump of motorcycle

lovely new bike back to a BSA dealer near you on a regular basis. Against this, the Rocket 3 was the fastest production bike readily available, handled well and stopped too.

Today, the package is better – but still much the same.

There is no argument that a sublimely restored Rocket 3, such as the one we had on test, is one of the most impressive classic motorcycles in the world. It's big, with a huge personality, and sits right alongside exotica like the Münch Mammut or MV Agusta America. Compared to the top hitters in the classic world, a truly top rate Rocket 3 is actually rather cheap at £15,000.

A well sorted triple is also one of the few classics capable of running right

alongside modern Retro bikes in terms of speed – certainly if you stay in licence retaining territory. So, there is much to like and a lot to recommend the Rocket 3 – and then there isn't.

The triple still has to be kicked into life, remains a four-speeder and is both wider and heavier than a Bonneville or Spitfire and these, despite whatever triple enthusiasts might argue, are facts.

So, for me, I would have a BSA Spitfire twin every day. The Spitfire is lighter, handles better, is virtually as fast and looks drop gorgeous too. And I'd enjoy looking at the £6000 I'd saved over the cost of a Rocket 3.

Thanks to Lawrence Rose, of Classic Motorcycles Ltd in Cheshire, for the loan of this truly stunning Rocket 3. ■

BMW R90S

THE COUNTRY EATER

For a few years I wrote a column based around motocross GPs, at a time when motocross ranked right alongside road racing as a strong news topic in all the magazines. It was a great job and involved a huge amount of travelling and a lot of time spent in very close contact with the teams and riders, which was fascinating.

Like MotoGP racing today, it was an intensely introspective world, where who won what and who did and didn't do something to someone else was more important than the plight of two million Biafrans who had starved to death in the Nigerian civil war five years earlier, or the UK's infamous 'three day week'. Maybe this narcissistic introspection was why I eventually fell out of love with reporting the minutiae of motocross.

Having said that, I did enjoy riding the length and breadth of Europe, often on BMW's magnificent R75/5 and, occasionally, when a bike was available from BMW GB's press fleet, the awesome R90S. »

"THE THREE ACES WHICH THE R90S HAD TO PLAY WERE USABILITY, FITNESS FOR PURPOSE AND TOTALLY UNBURSTABLE RELIABILITY."

The four gallon fuel tank meant that a lot of miles could be covered between refills

The R90 cockpit was incredibly sophisticated for its day

Ask a rider in the late 1960s what he thought of BMWs – girls virtually never rode motorcycles so I can use the pronoun 'he' with some certainty – and the response would have been along the lines that they were solid, reliable workhorses ridden by hard men who thought that using a plastic bag to sleep on in a blizzard was a sign of effete decadence.

BMWs of the period came in a wide range of colours. There was black, black, black and black. Customising a BMW meant painting it white. In those less enlightened times, and certainly for the characters we are talking about, white demonstrated a confused sexual orientation and was therefore very suspect.

Because BMW riders tended to like their bacon sandwiches still attached to the hind legs of a wild boar, which they could then bare-handedly fight to the death, and felt that consuming 10 gallons of weissbier before a ride was the least any real man could do, BMWs were started manually, courtesy of a tiny pedal attached to the rear of the gearbox. Mainstream humans failed miserably at this task but the Über Beings who rode BMWs could manage to fire up the Bavarian flat twins using no more than the end of their little finger or, in an emergency, perhaps the tip of their left ear lobe. In short, BMWs lacked mass market appeal. All this was about to change.

As the 1960s departed and the new, flower tied, flared jeaned and pink shirted 1970s were born, BMW hit the biking world with a range of truly outstanding motorcycles. And at the very top of this fresh, shiny tree was the R90S.

The R90S was one of the cleverest motorcycles ever to be produced and was proof positive that, deep in southern Germany, BMW's marketing team really understood the problem they faced. In addressing the factory's image of staid, dull reliability they managed to do that smartest of all three card tricks: retain their existing customers, bring in new ones – and do so cost effectively.

Technically, the R90S was light years behind the best of the Japanese and was nothing more than a modest technical step-up from earlier boxer twins. Thus the shaft drive was retained, as was the two-valve, horizontally opposed, push-rod twin cylinder engine. This was not state-of-the-art engineering by any stretch of the imagination. But what an engine the Germans produced. The new power-plant, with its five-speed gearbox, still looked, sounded and felt like previous BMWs but this was a motor which had been to the gym for a serious work out.

The three aces which the R90S had to play were usability, fitness for purpose and totally unburstable reliability. With a top speed of less than 120mph, the R90S lost out to the true hyper sports bikes of the day and was, on paper, no faster than Triumph's 750 Trident or the Honda CB750. The big difference was that the BMW's 120mph top speed equated to a solid 110mph cruising performance.

This point needs stressing. Riding an R90S it was comfortably, practically and realistically possible to cover 90 miles in an hour and 150-plus in two hours. Nothing else in the bike world, and very few cars of the time,

could offer this supreme distance devouring performance. Miles didn't disappear beneath the BMW's wheels – whole countries simply zipped past in a satisfying blur.

I used BMWs as my carriage of choice when I was reporting on Motocross GPs in the 1970s and 600 miles in a long, albeit pre-speed camera day, was not unusual. The 900 miles from San Marino to Calais was a bit of a haul… but only for me, not the Beemer.

Critics of the motor complained, justifiably, that the gearbox was dreadful compared with the Kawasaki Z1 – which it was. BSA Group triple owners boasted that their bikes offered vastly better handling, and this too was fairly true. And the supremely refined Honda CB750 was infinitely smoother. But when the BMW rider looked at his map and saw that there were 1500 miles of hard riding ahead there was always going to be just one winner.

The motor might have only produced 67hp, but what wonderfully practical, user friendly, willing and reliable horses they were.

A key element to the package was BMW's shaft drive. In the early 1970s, everyone who rode a big bike could adjust the rear drive chain at the side of the road. This skill was as essential as being able to open the filler cap on the fuel tank, and just as well understood.

Even so, it was a real nuisance. Ride a big, heavy, powerful bike – like Kawasaki's Z1 – hard and you would expect to adjust the chain maybe every 1000 miles and replace it every 5000.

Then there was the absolute necessity of spraying the chain with sticky lube which threw off all over the swinging arm… and on to the bottom of the rear panniers… and any pillion passenger who happened to be in the way.

If you wanted to say something about your status in 1970s' society the big Beemer was the way to do it

All this was tolerable for the recreational rider who was going to do a couple of hundred miles in a weekend, but not if you were on a mission. I wanted, and needed sometimes, to ride all day long until I was exhausted and to do this demanded the R90S' maintenance-free shaft drive.

The chassis complemented the motor wonderfully. The R90S was never the hyper-sports bike which BMW claimed but it was a supremely confident high speed performer. With 8in (208mm) of long travel suspension, superb rider ergonomics and a large, 5.27 gallon (25 litre) fuel tank, the bike allowed the rider to make use of the motor's abilities. As pilots of modern sports bikes know all too well, there is no point in having limitless performance if the riding position causes agony after 50 miles.

There was also a delightful attention to detail which inculcated a sense of pride in owning a BMW. As an example, the twin 10.6in (260mm) discs were drilled not only for lightness but also to enhance their performance in wet weather. So far, so good. What was really clever was that BMW first cadmium plated the disc, so that the drilled holes wouldn't rust, and then surface ground the rotors. Knowledgeable observers stood back, looked at the BMW and nodded sagely at the outstanding fit and finish. The R90S was expensive but looked to be an out and out bargain when compared with its British and Japanese opposition.

And last but not least, there was the R90S's appearance. In a deliberate attempt to put the black and dour images behind it, BMW produced its new flagship in a range of stunning, air brushed colours from burnt

> ## "THERE WAS ALSO A DELIGHTFUL ATTENTION TO DETAIL WHICH INCULCATED A SENSE OF PRIDE IN OWNING A BMW."

The R90S was designed for comfort and practicality and was a lovely place to spend 600 miles.

orange to a magnificent air burst grey.

The impact of the styling was immediate and dramatic. Suddenly, for the wealthy, the R90S became the bike to have. Film stars, chief executives and City of London bankers became BMW owners and, in doing so, opened up a whole new market for the Bavarian bikes.

Yet the really clever thing was that hard core BMW enthusiasts stayed with the factory because of the bike's mechanical prowess: truly, the hardest thing for any company to pull off.

Today, the R90S is one of the great aspirational motorcycles of the classic bike world, and the price reflects the bike's status. Expect to pay anything up to £12,000 for a fine example which is very, very cheap for what you get. A bonus is that BMW is rather proud of the bikes from this era so there is a good, if not perfect, supply of spares.

Our thanks to Keith Campbell at Hourglass Racing for the loan of his personal R90S for this story. ■

BSA D14 BANTAM SPORTS

A HAPPY LITTLE SOUL – BUT TOO LITTLE AND TOO LATE

Although I was a hard-core BSA fan – as was anyone with red, white and blue blood who raced motocross in the late 1960s – I was never very fond of BSA Bantams, even though they were still just in production when I began riding.

The problem was that Bantams were old-fashioned. Old blokes with old attitudes, and people who didn't know anything about motorcycles, rode Bantams and although I was starving poor I would rarely be seen on anything as dull and, yes that word again, old-fashioned as a Bantam. For heaven's sake, this would have made me only one step away from a packet of Woodbines and dominoes in the pub.

The one Bantam I did, sort of, like was the Bantam Sports. It was, and is, a real cheeky Jack Russell of a bike – which is why I still can't help but like it.

Not very far beneath the surface of the Bantam engine lurks a prewar DKW design

"TECHNICALLY, THE SPORTS BANTAM ALREADY BELONGED IN A MUSEUM AT THE TIME OF ITS LAUNCH IN 1967..."

Flat handlebars and chequered tape were all very café racerish but things had moved on by the time the Bantam Sports was launched

There are two ways of looking at the BSA Bantam Sports – and both are correct in fact and interpretation. The first is that the bike is a not very extensively updated version of the original Bantam launched in 1947 – and that was a direct lift from the prewar DKW design. Viewed in this way, the little BSA is a crude, outdated, poor performing embarrassment when compared with the automatic lubrication, six-speed, pocket rocket ship which Suzuki were selling at the time, in the form of their iconic T20.

But there is another view which can be taken of the bike. It is such a cheerful little thing, in both looks and riding experience, that it brings a smile to any rider's face. Technically, the Sports Bantam already belonged in a museum at the time of its launch in 1967 but like a good, solid Lancashire hotpot you can't help feeling satisfied with a big plateful.

Although BSA was around for about another six years before production folded – depending on how exactly one marks the final demise – by the late 1960s, things were already in a dire mess at the famous Small Heath factory.

The Japanese – with the huge advantage of a fiercely protected home market and therefore immense home sales to serve as a base for exports – had already captured the high ground in small capacity motorcycles.

Even the most fanatically loyal fans of British motorcycles were severely tempted by such wonderful little bikes as the Honda S90, and the bigger Benley and Dream models from the same factory. By the time that the 90mph Suzuki T20 hit the market in 1967, BSA had already decided that the factory's survival depended on the high profit, large capacity machines which sold particularly well in America.

However, BSA dealers still demanded an entry level bike and the factory's answer was the Bantam Sports. The problem was an almost complete lack of R&D funding so BSA engineers were instructed to cobble together the best they could – while spending virtually nothing on development or new tooling.

Incredibly, the Bantam had only just

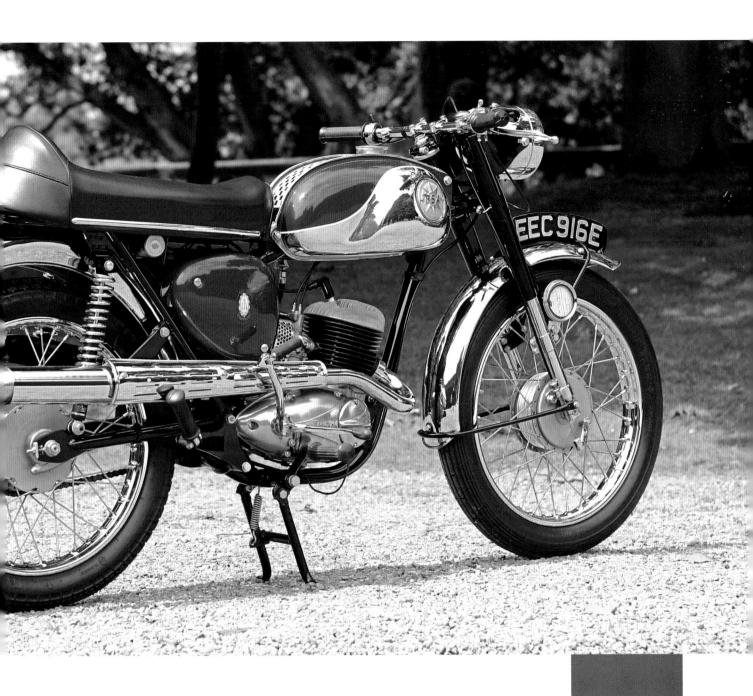

been given a four-speed gearbox and 12 volt electrics for the 1967 season but these two factors were a huge improvement over the three-speed box and six volts of a year earlier. The frame remained virtually unaltered, as did the dire front forks. BSA even had the temerity to sing the praises of the single leading shoe, full width hub which was lifted from the Triumph Tiger Cub. This, at a time when the Japanese supplied high quality, die cast, twin leading shoe brakes on virtually every bike they made.

The engine continued as very much a mirror version of the original, prewar DKW motor – even down to retaining the same 52mm stroke. Lubrication was still by pre-mix and this, perhaps more than anything else, crippled sales. Children of the Sixties, new to

motorcycling, simply did not take to the idea of removing a bottle of oil from a knapsack – usually an old, ex-Army gas mask bag – and then calculating the correct amount of lubricant for the fuel to be added to the tank. This was a prewar crudity that simply seemed out of place when the same customer merely filled up the oil tank on a contemporary Japanese two-stroke every 500 miles.

What made the situation even sadder is that BSA did have a Bantam with auto-lube ready for production but the management would not approve the extra £30 which the oiling system would have cost. Yet another example of the BSA directors being light years distant from their customers.

In order to get the Bantam Sports within a mile of its Japanese competition, BSA jacked »

Despite looking the part, the Bantam Sports is still a 1938 design and was far too little and too late to help BSA

With its high level exhaust, humped seat and lovely chrome, the Bantam Sports was a happy little bike. What a pity it was 10 years too late.

up the compression ratio of the D14 engine to 10:1. This raised the power to a claimed 12.5hp which resulted in an optimistic top speed of 65mph. To put this in perspective, when I started teacher training a few years later, I used a very well-worn Honda S90 as a runabout and the little Honda had about the same performance as the Beeza – despite being half its capacity. The big difference was that the Honda could be run flat out all day, every day. By contrast, any rider thinking about using the D14's supposed 65mph top whack really was tempting fate – not to say incurring loose fillings and a dose of white finger disease from the vibration.

The rise in compression ratio could cause pinking and/or seizures and the riveted flywheels were vulnerable as was the small end bearing. The Bantam's legendary frugality in terms of fuel consumption also suffered. BSA

fans, of which I was a cheerleader, claimed that the Small Heath bikes could still match the Japanese – but we were kidding ourselves.

The cycle parts show that the hard pressed designers had a truly gifted knowledge of BSA's parts inventory. The end result is that the Bantam emanates the sort of chirpy happiness of a terrier on a rat hunting expedition. In fact, all the bits work together so well that the casual observer would never know that few of them were produced uniquely for the Bantam Sports. Best of all, the Bantam truly captures the spirit of the café racer – lots of chrome, flat bars, humped seat – all the styling cues are there in abundance.

The problem is that the chassis wasn't up to handling the Bantam Sports' performance. Tyres were getting better all the time and the new generation of high grip rubber stressed the chassis dreadfully, and the front forks in

> ## "THE D14 WAS YESTERDAY'S BIKE, FROM A TIME WHEN RIDERS TREATED THEIR MACHINES WITH COURTESY AND RESPECT – AND WAS NOT FOR LONG-HAIRED, ROCK 'N' ROLL HIPPIES LIKE ME."

particular. Of course, I only ever rode Bantams flat out – as I did every other bike I sat on – and I can, quite clearly, remember seeing the front forks flex like a tuning fork round traffic islands with decent, grippy tarmac. The D14 was yesterday's bike, from a time when riders treated their machines with courtesy and respect – and was not for long-haired, rock 'n' roll hippies like me.

Today, despite all its technical deficiencies, the whole motorcycle works very well for such an old design. The simple piston ported engine starts first kick – especially if electronic ignition has been retro-fitted. The gearbox is sweet and light and there is a delightful burble from the 12bhp engine; 45-50mph cruising is comfortably possible – with a tiny bit more for emergencies. At these speeds, and ridden in a thoughtful, classic manner, the brakes are fine and the

chassis provides non-stressful handling.

If this bike had been trundling out of Small Heath in 1957 it would now be firmly established as a star in the British bike firmament. As it is, the Bantam Sports is an even stronger reminder of just how deep a hole BSA was busily digging for its soon to arrive funeral. So, that's the bad news.

The good news is that D14s sell really strongly. It's all very well for the great and the good, who own Vincent Black Shadows and DBD34 Gold Stars, to look down at the rest of us from on high, but the reality is that you can have a lot of affordable, simple and reliable pleasure on a D14. In the case of the D14 Sport, which really is a nice looking little bike, there is fun and a bit of low grade status too. However, this comes at a price and you can expect to pay north of £2500 for a really mint D14 Sports. ∎

Even when running well, it was never a good idea to use all the Bantam's performance which was fragile at best and often explosive when the flywheels came unriveted

THE BSA SPEEDWAY BIKE

A HUSH, HUSH (PUPPY) PROJECT

There are very few certainties in life: birth, death, taxes, the contact breaker spring flying across the workshop at midnight... and if you try to use Hush Puppy shoes to stop a bike from 60mph they will self-destruct. I know this for sure, because on one lovely spring day in 1973 I had to drive back from the BSA factory in Small Heath in my socks.

I like telling this story if only to show what was possible in pre Elfin Safety Britain. Here's the plot. Ride an unsilenced speedway bike through a busy factory at 60mph, with safety gear comprising of a tweed jacket and a pair of Hush Puppy shoes.

Was it reckless and stupid? Absolutely. Was it fun? More than you can imagine. And, if I had been there again, with all those lovely secretary girls cheering and giggling, would I have done it again? That's a silly question. Screaming safety officers, in their HiVis yellow vests and hard hats, wouldn't have kept me off that bike – although the lovely Cyril Halliburn, who built it, might well have done.

BSA Quality control shop –
source of many grey projects
including the speedway bike

There wasn't much to the BSA speedway bike

By 1973, BSA was in deep, deep trouble and things were happening at the factory that would have been unthinkable even two years before. It had always been BSA policy not to sell engines to anyone outside the company but now, every potential source of income was being hunted down.

One of the ideas was to manufacture both a complete BSA speedway bike, ready to race, and also to sell engines to riders. The Competition Shop had been closed the year before but there was still race development of sorts taking place at Small Heath. This was carried out by Cyril Halliburn, a dignified, archetypal Midlands engineer who was in charge of quality control at BSA. In his younger days, Cyril was known as 'Mr Gold Star' for his knowledge in tuning the renowned BSA singles and he was a keen racing enthusiast.

Cyril hatched the idea of taking the B.50 motocross engine and turning it into a speedway engine. From BSA management's point of view it had the dual benefits of being an extremely cheap project and one that might

well have shown some income very quickly.

The concept looked to be quite practical too. The very best B.50 motocross engines were giving around 39bhp while the B.50 road racer ridden by Bob Heath was up to nearly 45bhp – both running on 5 star (101 octane), pump petrol.

Jawa speedway engines, which were the standard equipment at the time for professional racers, produced 50bhp on methanol. Since methanol provides around a 25% increase in power over petrol, on paper, it looked as if the BSA would be a sound proposition.

The idea was that standard B.50 castings would be used for the cylinder barrel, head and rocker box and B.50 internals would also be employed. Only the crankcases would be new, since speedway engines had no need of a gearbox and conventional clutch.

The bikes were built in a tiny bay next to Cyril's office by Martin Russell and John Kay, who also worked on a few other 'grey' projects as well as undertaking their quality control duties. One of these was a variant of Martin's A65 twins for road racing and another was a »

"SINCE METHANOL PROVIDES AROUND A 25% INCREASE IN POWER OVER PETROL, ON PAPER, IT LOOKED AS IF THE BSA WOULD BE A SOUND PROPOSITION."

motocross bike ridden by me. Not that I had a works BSA on riding merit. At the time, I was writing two influential columns in American magazines and the motocross bike was a cost effective method of keeping in touch with me.

More than that, the people at BSA loved racing and if they had lost their works team then they had to make do with what was left – and if that was nothing more than a fanatically keen Clubman runner then this was better than not being involved in racing at all.

For my part, I was always conscious of the privileged position I occupied and was both grateful for BSA's help and respectful of the senior staff who gave it. As a result, I was allowed to wander around the factory almost at will, being patted on the head and played with, much in the manner of a favoured puppy.

One day I was summoned to meet Reg Dancer, who was the BSA Group's patrician PR manager ('Reg' to me) and Alistair Cave

– the BSA works' manager – who was very definitely 'Mr Cave'!

I had seen the BSA speedway bike on a number of occasions and was now asked for my opinion of its sales prospects. The bottom line was that Reg and Mr Cave wanted a cast iron assurance that they would sell a thousand engines before the project was started. The sting in the tail was that they wanted to stop development dead and not support any riders racing the BSA engines once the motors were sold.

Humbly, but forcefully, I tried to explain two things. First, that 1000 speedway engines was a huge number for the market to absorb bearing in mind that none of the former Iron Curtain countries would have purchased them. They all had to buy the Czech produced Jawas.

Second, you just can't sell a racing engine and walk away from it: there has to be constant development.

> I'm looking like a kid at Christmas because I've just persuaded Cyril to let me ride the speedway bike – inside the factory at Small Heath

"... SOON THE GIRLS IN THE NEW OFFICE BLOCK WERE HANGING OUT OF THE WINDOWS, CHEERING AND WAVING."

The speedway engine was not much more than the front of a B.50 motocross engine lightened and running on methanol

Reg and Mr Cave listened intently, asked lots of questions and made copious notes. Then I was released to go and play again.

Back in Quality Control I began badgering Cyril to let me ride the speedway bike, only to be met with a firm refusal. However, like all loving parents, Cyril eventually cracked and the bike was taken outside the factory. Now, the black and white truth is that there was absolutely nowhere to ride a speedway bike in what was a densely packed industrial site, but I didn't see this as a problem.

Added to this I didn't have any leathers, helmet or boots, just a sports jacket and my favourite Hush Puppies. But hey, this was the swinging Seventies and these were minor details. So Martin Russell cracked up the bike and soon the girls in the new office block were hanging out of the windows cheering and waving. And wasn't I a star works rider? And didn't my public demand a show? Well, there was only one answer...

I thought the first run was pretty good. Wind the motor up to 4000rpm, drop the clutch and the B.50 fairly tore alongside the factory wall with the noise from the straight pipe ricocheting off the windows like anti-aircraft fire. Even on the brakeless speedway bike, there was plenty of room to slow down and return to Cyril.

Mr Halliburn wanted me off the bike there and then, but the girls wanted more. This run was going to be the big one. 6000rpm, bang in the clutch and let the show begin. The back wheel spun for 10 yards and then hooked up and we tore alongside the building in the best possible style. 60mph was there in three seconds and then...

Well, the 'then' was a pallet truck full of castings. The driver took one look at the speedway bike bearing down on him and abandoned ship. I shut off, leaned forward and applied both Hush Puppies to the road. My legs buckled, bits of shoe flew everywhere but I just, and only just, stopped.

Cyril was a lovely man – gentle, patient and

kind. He looked at the flapping shoes for at least three seconds, said nothing and Martin returned the bike to Quality Control while I padded behind dejectedly. He didn't have to say anything; I knew. And so ended my career as a BSA speedway test rider.

As for the B.50, Arthur Browning rode it at a test at Coventry Speedway and declared it a no-hoper. "It just wasn't fast enough. A two valve Jawa would p*** all over it and using the same gearing as a Jawa, it wouldn't pull off the line. Professional riders would never have bought it, even if it was half the price of a Jawa."

The doors finally closed on BSA and the speedway engine died. Would it have ever been a success? Personally I doubt it, but it certainly gave me one of the most bowel loosening thrills of my riding career. ∎

The ever indulgent Cyril Halliburn, who designed the B.50 engined bike, and fitter Martin Russell who built it

THE DAY BSA DIED

I wrote this story for the first part of my autobiography, A Penguin in a Sparrow's Nest, and the memories still bring actual tears to my eyes. At the time, I was BSA's last works rider – not on merit but just because I was in the right place at the right time and knew how to say 'thank you'… and mean it.

My B.50 motocrosser was being rebuilt in the factory when my wife took a phone call from BSA. I didn't realise that three hours later I was going to be present at one of the seminal moments in the history of the British motorcycle industry… »

Until incompetent management killed the factory, BSA was a happy place to work

BSA suffered from being a city centre site but was very modern

Happy days with my works BSA. I was a Beezer man to the last drop of my blood

BSA was a worldwide brand right up to the moment the factory closed

"... IF THERE HAS EVER BEEN A FASTER TIME TO COVER 85 MILES TOWING A TRAILER I WOULD BE VERY SURPRISED."

On a lovely October day, Bill Weatherhead phoned my wife with an urgent message: BSA was going to close–and that day. If I didn't collect my B.50, it was certain that I would lose it: absolutely guaranteed!

This was a double tragedy, because clearly my career as BSA's last ever works rider was fast coming to an end… and I had bought the bike from the factory, so I was also going to lose my bike!

My wife rang me at school–and this was where working for a headteacher who was a bike racing fan really paid off.

Mr Teare came down to my class, explained what was happening and said: "Look, you'll be useless teaching today because you'll be worrying so much. I'll take your class and you go and rescue the BSA." Now that was real kindness.

I said a very hurried goodbye to my class and screamed away from school, heading for home to collect my trailer.

On the grounds that I might still incriminate myself after all these years, I will say only that if there has ever been a faster time to cover 85 miles towing a trailer I would be very surprised.

My wife had also phoned Bill Weatherhead to tell him that I was on my way and so the B.50 was leaning against the tubes, just by the exit to the Tubes In bay, when I arrived. We loaded the bike on to the trailer in seconds.

But Bill wasn't finished yet. He grabbed an enormous cardboard box and we ran down the B.50 assembly line. Into it went valves, two barrels, a couple of cylinder heads,

five pistons and much more. It was like one of the 'All You Can Grab in a Minute' supermarket competitions.

We were out of breath when we reached the end of the line. "How much have you got with you? Quick!" panted Bill.

"I've got 10 quid–but that's all."

"Give it me! Give it me now! Quick!" Bill barked.

I gave him the two £5 notes and he scribbled a receipt for me: "Assorted BSA spares–£10."

"Go on, get out now. Go on, go on, go on. Get out now."

I ran across to my car, which I had reversed up to the Tubes In bay and so was pointing in the right direction to leave the factory. Spinning the wheels, I accelerated towards the security cabin by the gate while, behind me, a group of blue suited men were descending the steel stairs from the new offices.

The security guard looked at the B.50 on the trailer and hesitated. "It's mine. Honestly, it's mine. Cyril Halliburn looks after it for me and Bill Weatherhead has just sold me some spares. I'm Frank Melling and the B.50's mine–honest…"

There were tears welling in my eyes. The guard looked at the huge box of parts on the back seat and then back at me.

"Look, I've got a receipt. Bill has just sold the bits to me, honest he has, honestly. Look at the receipt."

The suits had reached the bottom of the stairs by now and the factory gates were just a few seconds' walk away. »

"THERE WERE TEARS WELLING IN MY EYES. THE GUARD LOOKED AT THE HUGE BOX OF PARTS ON THE BACK SEAT AND THEN BACK AT ME..."

The guard looked at the bike, back at the BSA box with parts spilling out everywhere and then at my ashen face. Finally, and with what felt like infinite slowness, he took the receipt and waved me through.

I was shaking like a leaf and pulled up across the road, at the head of Golden Hillock Road, just to calm down. I was panting for breath and flopped forward across the steering wheel completely exhausted.

I raised my head and looked out of the driver's side car window across towards Armoury Road. The suited gentlemen from Cooper Brothers Accountants were locking the gates to the factory.

That was the end of BSA. ■

Riding my magnificent works BSA. What an honour for a Clubman rider of no great merit

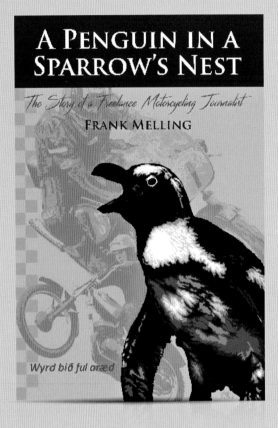

The Ducati Classic 1000 is a handsome motorcycle by any standards. Pity it was too early for its own good

DUCATI SPORT CLASSIC GT 1000

RIGHT BIKE, RIGHT PLACE, WRONG TIME, RIGHT TIME, WRONG TIME, RIGHT TIME ETC

This was a really strange article to write and I need to explain the rather special relationship I have with Carol – who is my wife, my best friend, the love of my life and my business partner too. She is also infinitely generous, unselfish and kind so, on the rare occasions when she wants something, really wants it, I can't wait to oblige. This is how we went to write a story about a very interesting bike… and ended up owning it. »

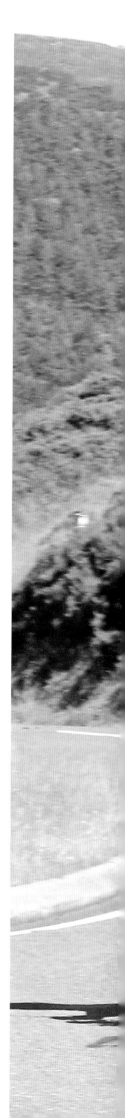

Timing is everything in a battle – military or sales. Initiate actions too late and you will be on the back foot. Commit your resources too early, they will be wasted – and you will lose. Nowhere is this adage more apparent than with the Ducati Sport Classic range.

The Classics owe their birth to a series of fortunate, or maybe unfortunate, circumstances for the Bologna factory and the story is a fascinating one.

At the epicentre of the tale is Pierre Terblanche, the South African born – but internationally domiciled – designer who engenders unequivocal responses whenever his work is seen in public. Terblanche fans rate Pierre as one of the great motorcycle designers of all time with a string of iconic motorcycles to his name... such as the first Ducati Multistrada, the MH900E Ducati and the Confederate X132 Hellcat Speedster.

His critics point to the universally reviled Ducati 999, which was bland compared with the genius of the 916, to show what happens when the South African misses the mark.

Pierre is a Mike Hailwood fan and, born in 1956, is old enough to remember the classic era of motorcycle racing. Having, nearly, been there when this wonderful period of motorcycle racing was taking place, the sights, sounds and the very feel of these evocative motorcycles are woven into his DNA. This is an important factor in the Ducati Classic story.

In homage to Hailwood, and his 1978 TT winning 900SS Ducati, Terblanche penned the MH900E for Ducati in September 1998. The bike was a sort of café racer tribute bike – or something along those lines – and immediately elicited rave reactions both from the press and Ducatisti.

I was at the head of the queue praising the bike for its style, originality and honesty. The E stood for 'evoluzione' and was a really clever interpretation of what a Ducati 900SS might have looked like 20 years on from Hailwood's legendary win.

Ducati tested the market with a web survey and, on the basis of the positive response, the factory decided to take a chance on the radical new bike and produce 2000 units. However, Ducati's CEO at the time, Massimo Bordi, was still nervous about the project so decided to protect the company's back by selling the MH directly from Bologna and just giving dealers a pdi and delivery fee for handling the new motorcycle.

Sales opened on January 1, 2000 at 00:01 GMT with a price of €15,000 – which was a lot of money at the time.

The first 1000 units were sold out in just over half an hour and the rest of the production run went in a couple of weeks.

Clearly retro was hot, Terblanche could deliver the styling goods, and a brand new money tree had just popped up in Ducati's income orchard.

With the benefit of hindsight I didn't possess at the time, I think that it was the Mike Hailwood name which led Ducati astray.

Like so many other motorcyclists of my generation I worshipped Hailwood and, had I not been re-building my life after some very severe financial challenges, I would have been logging into Ducati's website desperate to put my €15,000 down to own a piece of Hailwood memorabilia.

When I took delivery of my MH I would have stroked, polished and loved it, but the motoart would have probably seen very little time on the road. In this respect, I was an archetypal MH900E customer.

Fast forward to the 2003 Tokyo Motorcycle Show and Ducati appeared with another radical Terblanche concept, this time for Retro motorcycles and doffing the cap of nostalgia towards Paul Smart's 1972 Imola 200 win.

The new bikes were fairly hard core café racer styled machines, complete with low handlebars and rear set footrests, which demanded a committed riding stance. That's the classic DNA dominating Terblanche's pen once again.

The new bikes were well received – particularly by the media, who didn't have to buy them!

So the middle-aged, but amply funded, wended their way into Ducati showrooms all over the world, test rode the new bike on their own and then returned with aching knees and numbed wrists.

And yes, I was one of them.

Meanwhile, their life partner had been drumming her fingers on the Ducati salesman's desk wondering what her part in the proceedings would be – other than signing off the cheque. »

"CLEARLY RETRO WAS HOT, TERBLANCHE COULD DELIVER THE STYLING GOODS, AND A BRAND NEW MONEY TREE HAD JUST POPPED UP IN DUCATI'S INCOME ORCHARD."

A warm, sunny day, empty mountain road and a GT1000. Motorcycling does not get any better

"IN THE REAL WORLD, THE ENGINE IS A PEACH – TORQUEY, POWERFUL AND WITH A VERY ANTHROPOMORPHIC THROB: AUTHENTICALLY CLASSIC AND YET THOROUGHLY MODERN."

If the lady was motorcycle minded, the price of the Classic had also come to her attention. If she liked Ducatis, the company would sell the couple the fast, comfortable, sophisticated ST Tourer for almost an identical price to the Sport. Triumph's insipid Bonneville was much cheaper and more practical, if the pair wanted to go down the still nascent Retro route. Just as importantly, the Bonnie was over £2500 cheaper than the Duc–and that's a lot of money in the purely recreational end of the motorcycle market.

There was another problem–and a major one too. Riders migrating from Supersports bikes to the Bonneville, often because they were drinking in the last chance saloon in terms of retaining their licence, were full of praise for its mild, inoffensive, law-abiding power.

Equally, classic bike owners liked the Bonneville because its performance was not much better than a good British classic motorcycle, if at all.

By contrast, the Ducati Classic was most certainly not dull. With a 92hp V-twin engine housed in a package weighing only 407-and-a-bit pounds (185kg), the new Duc was very frisky–much more so than even the sportiest genuine old bike. This was not a motorcycle which middle-aged, ever thickening waist and thinning hair customers recognised at all.

At the same time, sports riders coming from Fireblades and 999s looked at 92hp with contempt. 92hp and 130mph? That's disability scooter territory!

The handling was out of sync with its time. For a start, instead of faking a classic bike with 18in wheels, the Classics came with 17 inchers laced on to sports bike wide rims. 43mm, upside down Marzocchi forks were not paying homage to anything produced by Ducati post Imola–and even less to a classic British bike.

None of this meant Ducati did not understand, in a very intimate way, how the bike should handle. With a steering head angle of 24° and 103mm of trail, the Classic was balanced perfectly on the edge of sports bike steering geometry. Another 1° steeper head angle, and a tiny bit less trail, and you are into counter-steering and all the other modern sports bike nonsense. As things stood, the handling was race track steady while remaining utterly intuitive and neutral.

The brakes also caused eyeballs to pop out on prospective customers. There were no single discs or drums here. On the contrary, a pair of walloping great Brembo 230mm anchors lived up front and an equally impressive 240mm disc was at the rear.

Clearly, where the Classics fitted perfectly was in a brand-new category–the 'Supersports Retro'. Sadly for Ducati, this slot didn't exist at the time!

The problem for Ducati was that by this point in the project, serious money had been invested in the new bikes. At the heart of the range was the best ever air cooled motor produced by the boys from Bologna. The new, six speed engine was 992cc and produced a very acceptable 92hp @ 8000rpm and a just as impressive 67.2lb-ft (91.1Nm) of torque at a mere 6000rpm.

Ducati spent a lot of cash developing the power plant to make it efficient and Euro 3 compliant with a huge amount of effort going

Faux analogue clocks look lovely and hide some key digital information

into the cylinder head, which has a very narrow valve angle, together with a new combustion chamber shape and much shortened exhaust tract. These changes, plus 45mm Marelli electronic fuel injectors feeding each short stroke 94mm x 71.5mm cylinder, and twin spark ignition, allow the motor to run very lean and yet still efficiently.

In the real world, the engine is a peach – torquey, powerful and with a very anthropomorphic throb: authentically classic and yet thoroughly modern. The six speed gearbox is faultless and the hydraulic clutch rider friendly and progressive.

In fact, Ducati hit the dead centre of the target with this engine. All that was missing was a mass appeal chassis.

Enter then, in 2006, the GT – the first bike Ducati should have made in the Classic range. Gone is the rather affected, single sided swinging arm of the Paul Smart rep, and the café racer riding position of the Classic Sport, to be replaced by a traditional twin sided design and much more upright riding position. The divorce inducing single seat was shown the door, to be replaced by a truly lovely dual saddle. Relocating the footrests, and raising the bars, meant that the ergonomics became instantly rider friendly.

Not that the new bike lacked anything in terms of handling or performance. The chassis was a close sibling of the café racer's and the brakes and motor were identical. How good was the handling? In 2008, I was very much on Ducati's Christmas card list and so I got an invitation to ride in its TT celebration with a lap of the TT course on closed roads – and with no speed control. The old GP bike I was supposed to ride 'phoned in sick' and so the only thing available was a Classic GT, and I can report that the handling is sublime at 100mph-plus – all the way to unintentionally touching »

> I rode a Sport Classic around the TT course on a parade lap and it was brilliant at really ludicrous speeds

"THEN A STRANGE THING HAPPENED. THE WORD SLOWLY, VERY SLOWLY, GOT AROUND AMONG DUCATISTI THAT THE SPORT CLASSICS WERE WORTH HAVING."

The Paul Smart
version of the
Sport Classic
did a lot to put
customers off
the Retro idea

down the right-hand silencer at Sulby Bridge!

I was so impressed with the bike that, once more, I nearly bought one.

'Nearly' was the key adverb because a lot more customers for the Ducati Sport Classics almost, but not quite, got out their wallets... and 'nearly' doesn't pay the bills. Retro, complete with faded, fake t-shirts and lifestyle accessories hadn't quite yet come to town and so the GT, and its siblings, were just slow, old fashioned, modern motorcycles.

With sales grinding to a halt, production was stopped in 2010 and the bike entered a dark and gloomy backwater. If you wanted a cheap Retro/modern Ducati Classic, this was the time to buy one.

Ironically, the winter of 2010 was just the time when the youngsters discovered Retro.

Andrew Woods, of Woods Motorcycles, is a long standing Ducati dealer. He remembers the situation well: "We had plenty of customers test ride the Classic but they never bought them. The problem was that there were many other bikes you could get for the same money.

"The Sport was also uncomfortable. Your bum was stuck up in the air and the clip ons were far too low. The saddle height was also too high. Compared with a Triumph Bonneville, this wasn't a bike you could imagine riding all day... for the very good reason that you couldn't ride it all day without getting off crippled!

"In the end we discounted them, as every Ducati dealer in Britain did, just to get rid.

"Ducati should have launched the range with the Paul Smart and the GT, which is really comfortable, and then brought out the Sport later.

"The odd thing was that the people who did buy Classics loved the bikes, particularly the GT, but there just weren't enough of them to keep the range in production."

The road to anonymity was helped by the fact that even owners of the GT version of the Classic didn't ride them very much, so the bikes weren't even seen out in public sufficiently to generate a critical mass of interest.

This is a shame because an alternative way of viewing the £7495 selling price is that Ducati had provided a motorcycle of stunning quality. For example, very few production motorcycles can match the quality of the paintwork. Each fuel tank was hand sprayed and then flatted down four times before leaving the production line.

The attention to detail is sublime, with a polished alloy top fork yoke and a truly magnificent alloy bracket for the front mudguard on which all the weld puddles can be seen, just like a classic thoroughbred.

For me, the attention to detail and finish of the bike are what make it special. Terblanche almost, but not quite, got the overall look perfect too. Walk round the bike and it is catch-your-breath beautiful from every angle – except one. Why there is such a huge gap between the rear wheel and the mudguard is beyond me. »

The DS 1000
engine manages
to feel classic
and modern

Out on the road, the GT is superb, very involving but without the constant worry of licence-losing speeds.

With peak torque at 6000rpm it's an easy, relaxing ride and, even two up, hills are dismissed with contempt. Like all Ducatis, it's over geared for radar and laser monitored Britain and the GT needs a one-tooth smaller gearbox sprocket to keep the motor in the sweet spot at legal speeds. In fact, Ducati recognised this and offered the smaller gearbox sprocket as an accessory.

Being a V-twin, with the weight concentrated narrowly along the centre line, the bike feels lighter than it is, even with a full four gallons of fuel, which the GT sips at a miserly 50mpg plus.

Relaxed cruising speed is 80mph and it will zip up to this with ease and enthusiasm. The ergonomics are excellent with a near perfect riding position for me at 5ft 10in. The saddle is thick and supportive and there is plenty of wriggle room for Carol on the pillion too.

Being light and slim, the GT is also city centre friendly and ideal for lane splitting.

The standard silencers emit a lovely, deep Ducati throb and why anyone should think that fitting aftermarket cans to a GT, and so annoying everyone in the process, is utterly

beyond me. In fact, it's the perfect bike for the 21st century.

Then a strange thing happened. The word slowly, very slowly, got around among Ducatisti that the Sport Classics were worth having.

The first bike in the range to go collector priced ballistic was the Paul Smart. There were only 2000 of these built to begin with, and it didn't require much interest to hike up the price. However, there is a vast difference between what greedy owners, and dealers, think that they can get for PS Classics and what money actually changes hands. £15,000 will still buy a mint PS but there is no doubt that prices are rising steeply.

The situation is the same for the Sport and GT models too, with a fair sprinkling of avaricious vendors hoping for an easy hit.

Not that the story is over quite yet.

By 2015, the Retro market was on fire – led by Triumph's excellent Bonneville range. With the arrival of the Triumph Thruxton R the GT was back in the frame, not as a collector's bike but rather as a legitimate motorcycle to own and ride in its own right.

Here's where things become very interesting indeed. The GT is a direct competitor for a standard Thruxton R, except that it is

> The GT is not only a fine Retro but an excellent modern bike too

better in many ways. The performance is very similar – even down to the fuel consumption – and the handling is just as good. The Triumph brakes better but there is very, very little to choose between the two bikes.

Where the GT wins hands down is that it is a vastly more practical motorcycle. The Duc has a dual seat as standard and the riding position is much more sensible. It's also an expensive exercise to get a Thruxton R into GT trim. Finally, it is currently possible to buy a really nice GT for half the price of a Thruxton. In fact, all of the Ducati Classic range is available to be bought at a sensible price, especially if you have cash to put down on the table rather than taking a part exchange into a dealer.

So, don't be put off by the apparent 'collectors' prices' you will see advertised and don't be persuaded by the argument that you can never lose money on a Ducati Classic, because the actors for what may be the final act in the saga are currently in the wings, waiting to come on to the stage.

In 2014, Ducati launched its own Retro with the Scrambler range of bikes, and these became an immediate best seller. However, the one thing which was missing was a 1000cc café racer. When the new bike appears, as it most certainly will, the Ducati Classic range will immediately fade into becoming just nice, old bikes... so if

you are thinking about selling your Duc Classic, now is the time to do it. If you are going to buy one, and are price conscious, wait a while until the Scrambler range has a challenger for the Thruxton R.

And now for a final, personal, postscript to this story.

Carol and I had decided that we didn't need, or really want, another road bike. We were a racing couple and the race paddock, with our race bike, is where we naturally live. Equally we had never, since we first met, been without a road bike.

I wanted to write a story about a Ducati Classic GT so we called in at a dealer who had one for sale to refresh my memory. The GT sat there – 10 years old, gleaming red and with just 3500 miles on the odometer. Carol was smitten on the spot. Then she sat on the saddle and fell utterly and totally in love. Ten minutes later, a spot of informal research had become a sale... and that doesn't happen many times in a motojournalist's career!

Just 3000 miles later, the GT has been one of the best motorcycle purchases I have ever made. It's everything I want as a solo rider and perfect for us as a riding couple, and it saved us £6000 over the cost of a new Thruxton R.

As for price increases or falls – we're having too much fun to be bothered. ■

> The MH900E Ducati was the bike which convinced Ducati that money could be made from Retros

Getting the Norton to start wasn't straightforward. Here's George Cohen pushing like crazy while I juggle all the controls

RIDING THE 1907 TT-WINNING NORTON

WHEN HEROES RACED

Sometimes, the sense of privilege at being a motojournalist, as distinct from having a real job, strikes home hard. It did so as I approached the 1907 TT-winning Norton, which the National Motorcycle Museum was going to let me ride.

This motorcycle dates from a period only 74 years after the abolition of slavery in the British Empire. It was a time when personal safety, and life, was cheap and getting killed in accidents simply a fact of normal, everyday life. The Norton was a true time machine back to a period which would horrify most people today.

The story has a sad postscript because a key person in making the test happen was the wonderfully eccentric George Cohen, the world's greatest authority on prewar Nortons, who has now sadly passed away. George was one of a kind, a genuine, authentic person and I liked him tremendously.

Ride well in heaven George – the angels' flat tank Nortons will be going a lot better now that you are tuning them.

»

aimed the Norton downhill, pedalled furiously and dropped the decompressor lever. The riveted leather belt slipped momentarily and then the rear wheel began to turn over the 672cc V-twin engine. The first sounds were a dull, asthmatic wheezing, then a hesitant stutter and finally a glorious, hard edged crackle as the 100-year-old engine burst into life. A touch more fuel and time's opaque curtains were torn to shreds as the Norton accelerated aggressively through the damp, early evening mist – and I was transported back almost a century to Rem Fowler's, and Norton's, win in the first ever TT.

Arguments rage over what was the first ever motorcycle so it's easier to say that 10 years before the Norton, the sporting young man would have certainly been on a horse; motorcycles were virtually unknown and racing non-existent. It is in this context that the TT-winning Norton needs viewing.

James Lansdowne Norton was a keen

competitor from the moment he began building his very first motorcycles in the back streets of Birmingham and ardently believed in racing as a sales tool. The 1907 concept of racing was not quite as we understand it today. The central ideas which drove the early competitors, and manufacturers, were reliability, fuel consumption and the ability to ascend hills – with or without pedal assistance.

Because late 19th century England was the most heavily industrialised nation in the world, the authorities had extensive knowledge of powered vehicles in the form of traction engines – and they didn't like them. In 1896, the final version of the Locomotive Act was introduced – and racing on closed public roads was effectively banned forever. Well, not quite forever because just as I am writing this chapter it has become legal to run races for cars and bikes on British public roads but none have so far taken place.

This didn't stop the infant motorcycle

"BY 1907 STANDARDS, THE NORTON WAS CUTTING EDGE TECHNOLOGY AND FEATURED SEVERAL STATE-OF-THE-ART FEATURES."

The Norton was both crude and state-of-the-art sophistication for 1907. It was also fast!

industry from wanting to go racing. Rather, it meant that the show had to be moved offshore.

The Isle of Man was the perfect venue. At one end was Liverpool, one of England's biggest ports, with all of the infrastructure needed to handle cargo. Eighty miles away was a sparsely populated island, complete with a mountain, where the authorities welcomed tourists of any kind and were more than happy to close roads for any kind of motorsport – and still are for that matter.

The first motorcycle race was held on May 28, 1907, over 10 laps of the Short Course which was 15 miles and 1470 yards beginning in the village of St John's in the west of the island. It was for road-legal, touring motorcycles with exhaust silencers, saddles, pedals and mudguards.

Twenty-five riders started in pairs, racing on largely unsurfaced roads. In the damp and mist of that May morning, 'Pa' Norton and his top rider Rem Fowler brought the Norton to the start line.

The bike is a strange mixture of contradictions. It is clearly a full sized motorcycle with a 60in (1524mm) wheelbase, which is impressive even by today's standards. Equally, it looks to be dangerously, almost maniacally, flimsy. The frame and front forks »

"THE TRANSMISSION IS SIMPLICITY IN ITSELF: THERE ISN'T ANY!"

are pure, unadulterated bicycle; no ifs and buts. This is a traditional, brazed lug construction bicycle into which someone has shoehorned a neat, 45°, V-twin engine.

By 1907 standards, the Norton was cutting edge technology and featured several state-of-the-art features. Most notable of these was the Bosch magneto which reliably produced a spark to ignite the fuel. The magneto is driven by an open chain which whizzes round just in front of the pilot's right boot. Truly, this is a machine with which the rider feels intimately involved!

The Brown and Barlow carburettor was also a new concept. Air and fuel still have to be manually adjusted by the rider but can be done accurately, allowing unprecedented performance – for 1907.

The Peugeot V-twin engine has a mechanically operated exhaust valve and atmospherically

lifted inlet valve. This means that the exhaust is opened by cam, in the conventional manner, but suction from the piston driving down the cylinder opens the inlet valve. The received wisdom of the time felt that this was the route to efficient engine performance.

However, there were sceptics even at the turn of the century. Norton works rider Rem Fowler doubled the strength of the valve springs on the inlet valve from 4lb-ft to 8lb-ft. This cost him low down performance but enabled the V-twin to rev reliably to over 4000 rpm.

Lubrication is by a hand pump which forces oil into the engine where it finds its own way round the motor. The incredible lubricity of the heavy, castor based oil allows the engine to function very happily – blowing out the surplus at random, all over the road and verges.

George Cohen, who was the world's leading expert on early Nortons and the restorer of this bike, estimated that the Fowler machine gives around 12bhp, a figure which would make it a real MotoGP bike of its day.

The transmission is simplicity in itself, there isn't any! A large, riveted, four-ply leather belt

> **TT winner Rem Fowler and his pit crew – hard men one and all**

goes from the front engine pulley and drives the rear wheel. Disconcertingly, this heavy, thick and extremely breakage prone device whizzes past the rider's left calf. Health and safety legislators would love it.

There is no clutch either, so the drive is permanently engaged. This needs stressing. Once the motor is running forward momentum is maintained, unless the engine is stopped via the decompressor. Riding this bike is not for the faint-hearted.

Two, tiny bicycle brakes make a symbolic gesture at stopping the bike – but nothing more. In practice they have no effect and the best way to slow down is by pitching the bike sideways, pulling in the decompressor and putting down a boot.

To understand the Norton, it is important to see the bike in historical context. In 1907, half of all babies born into working class families died at birth and 10 year olds could still be legally employed in British factories. In this context, the lack of brakes and permanently engaged drive are not so much lethally dangerous – which they are – but part of a society where extreme personal injuries were the norm, rather than aberrant exceptions.

This makes Rem Fowler's achievement all the more exceptional. Despite a catalogue of

problems, including six spark plug changes, twice stopping to shorten the drive belt and a puncture repair, he set the fastest lap at 42.91mph – and this was on dirt roads sprayed with acid to reduce the dust. In doing so, Rem displayed the sort of premeditated, stoic courage which exemplified the Victorian age.

For weeks before writing this article, I had looked at the picture of Rem's hard, racer's face surrounded by his cocky, cigarette smoking mechanics and tried to imagine what it must have been like to line up at the first TT 100 years ago. Even though I race classic motorcycles today, the task was beyond me. My bikes turn and stop and accelerate like slow versions of modern racing machines. They are as safe as the rider wants to make them.

Rem's bike was inherently, overtly dangerous then – and is now. My nervousness was compounded by the bike's financial value. It is owned by the National Motorcycle Museum and the museum's founder, Roy Richards, had given special dispensation for me to ride it. Crashing, or even damaging, the bike was beyond contemplation. How do you replace a bike which is beyond value?

George pushed, I pedalled and the ancient Norton burst into life. Immediately, there is a lot to do. The Somerset lanes on which I rode »

I'm looking more than a bit tense in the picture because on the outside of the lane is a great, big stone wall and I can't stop the Norton. Neeeaaagh!

1907 Norton TT winner is a handsome beast in all its Pioneer glory

were a good replica of the early TT course and the first thing that is worrying – terrifying even – is the acceleration. Weighing only 182lb, the Norton picks up its skirts and accelerates in a manner which is galaxies away from the normal 'dumpty-dumpty-dumpty' of a plodding Pioneer bike. This is a real racing bike with all the edgy eagerness of a thoroughbred.

The bike skitters and slides all over the place and so the technique is simply to aim it. This is fine until a corner arrives and then things become really challenging. There are no brakes, the motor runs on and the 26in tyres don't grip on the shale and stones. And all this is at pedestrian speeds. Imagining what it must have been like at the 60mph Rem rode at is just too much for me.

All too soon, George was frantically waving me back. Carol said that she had never seen me more nervous on a test before and my sense of relief at the bike's return was palpable. For my part, I would have loved to have the Norton on a racetrack but I returned the bike deeply grateful for one of the most memorable experiences in 40 years of riding race bikes – and not a little relieved that the National Motorcycle Museum was not going to send me a £500,000 repair bill. ■

In a straight line, the Norton was fast and fun. The problems came with stopping or turning the beast!

FRANK KEEPS A CLOSE EYE ON A PACKET OF RICE, ORGANISES THE WORLD'S BIGGEST MOTORCYCLING STREET PARTY AND PROVES, ONCE AGAIN, THAT ANYTHING IS POSSIBLE IF YOU WANT IT HARD ENOUGH – EVEN GETTING A PENGUIN TO FLY!

The Flying Penguin has become an instant best seller and continues to attract readers throughout the world. Here's what readers think:

Broken bones, broken bikes, broken relationships – all precariously balanced on the knife-edge of a freelance journalist's permanent state of financial insecurity.

It's all told with disarming honesty and plenty of wit. Motorcycling enthusiasts will find much to entertain them – but there's also more meat to this man's life than just the two-wheeled side of things, so several chapters are dedicated to Frank's endeavours in education and literacy. He's also a dedicated family man, as you'll discover.

Out of the (occasionally all too real) fires of experience emerges, if not a phoenix then certainly, a Flying Penguin.
Rowena Hoseason
Real Classic magazine

My wife bought me this at the Stafford Show because I had so much pleasure from Frank's first book. This is a fitting follow on to book one as the motorcycling adventures come thick and fast, with lots of details about The Thundersprint which Frank paints in no holds barred detail for us. Somehow my copy seemed to have been treated with some form of drug as at the end of each chapter the book seemed to want me to move on to the next one without putting it down, so congratulations on a great read and maybe you will find the time in your busy life to write more books Frank.
Chris F

Even if you are not into bikes... read this book! Well written, great tales and a real sense of connection with everyday [and some not!] scenarios. Made me smile in a wet and cold January 2017! Will be taking this book and its prequel on holiday. Worth every penny
A C Patten

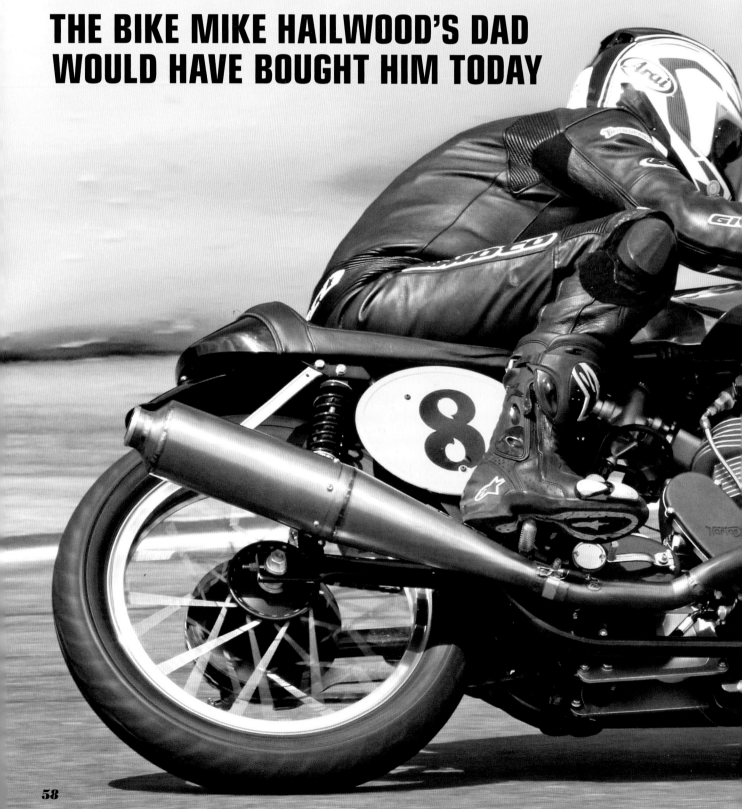

ECURIE SPORTIVE
MANX NORTON

THE BIKE MIKE HAILWOOD'S DAD WOULD HAVE BOUGHT HIM TODAY

When I do book signings there are always a lot of people wanting to tell me about the book they have nearly written, which is going to be vastly better than anything I have ever produced.

It's the same if you stand next to someone who has never raced. You'll hear all the trackside analyses about this rider being on the wrong line and that one who isn't trying. Truly, the track does look different on the spectator side of the Armco!

And let's not forget about the worst culprits of all—motojournalists who spend all their time giving opinions about whether this bike performs well or those gloves are any good.

The key question is whether we armchair critics could actually do any better? Given a blank sheet of paper, what would our results be?

There's a racing expression I love. It's this: "When the flag drops, the bull**** stops!"

With the Ecurie Sportive Manx project, I was about to find out whether I could actually style a bike – or not. And there would be no committee, editor or project planner to blame if I made a mess of things.

Here's what happened when I designed a race bike entirely on my own – and paid for the results. The one thing I know now, for sure, is that the job is a lot harder than it looks from the outside! »

One of the reasons I love riding motorcycles so much is that they give me the time and space to play my favourite cognitive game – undisturbed by phones, emails or even conversations with another human. There's just me, the bike and "What if…"

What if Miltiades, and his Athenian hoplites, had not held the road at Marathon in 490BC? Would the whole of Europe now have a Persian flavour?

What if Hitler had turned east, instead of west, in 1939 and, trampling the Soviet Union, had built a new German Empire?

And, most interestingly of all, if the world today was more or less as it was in 1960, what Norton would Stan Hailwood have provided for the up and coming, but not yet superstar, Mike?

Probably the only other person in the world even vaguely interested in analysing this last question is Patrick Walker – engineering genius and the sole employee of Works Racing Motorcycles and who builds the finest replica Manx Norton motorcycles in the world. So, as we sat outside Patrick's van, I explained the background story to the 1960/61 Hailwood Manx Norton…

Stan Hailwood was managing director of Kings of Oxford which was, by far, the biggest and most professional chain of motorcycle and car retailers in Britain with more than 50 branches in 1960. In short, he was both a millionaire and very well connected.

Before the Second World War, Stan had dabbled at motorcycle racing but was much more successful in car competition, racing a works prepared MG at Brooklands. It was there, at the famous Surrey concrete speedbowl, that he met Bill Lacey – a name central to this story.

As Hailwood's responsibilities at Kings grew, his competition days were brought to a close – but not his ambition to be the very best in racing – even if this dream had to be fulfilled through his son.

Enter then, centre stage, W G (Bill) Lacey who was one of the greatest Brooklands motorcycle racers of all time. In August 1928 he had won the Motor Cycle Trophy for the first British rider to average over 100 miles in an hour on a British track, when he thundered round Brooklands in the saddle of a Grindley Peerless JAP at an average of 103mph. On the rough, concrete circuit that would be fast on a modern Superbike. In 1928, the speed was simply science fiction rapid.

Later, Lacey – partnered by Wal Phillips – racked up 306 miles in three hours and riding solo he covered 110 miles in the hour at Montlhéry in France. In short, he was blisteringly quick.

Not only was Lacey a star rider but he was the finest tuner of his generation, preparing all his record-breaking machines himself.

Lacey's speciality – obsession is more accurate – was reliability. Concentrating on the double overhead cam Norton Manx engine, he carried out major modifications to improve the robustness of the main bearing and then applied meticulous assembly to the rest of the engine.

Not that he was against what was then state-of-the-art technology because Lacey experimented with twin plug ignition, chrome

From left: Bill Lacey, Mike Hailwood, Jim Adams and Stan Hailwood.
Image: Mortons Archive

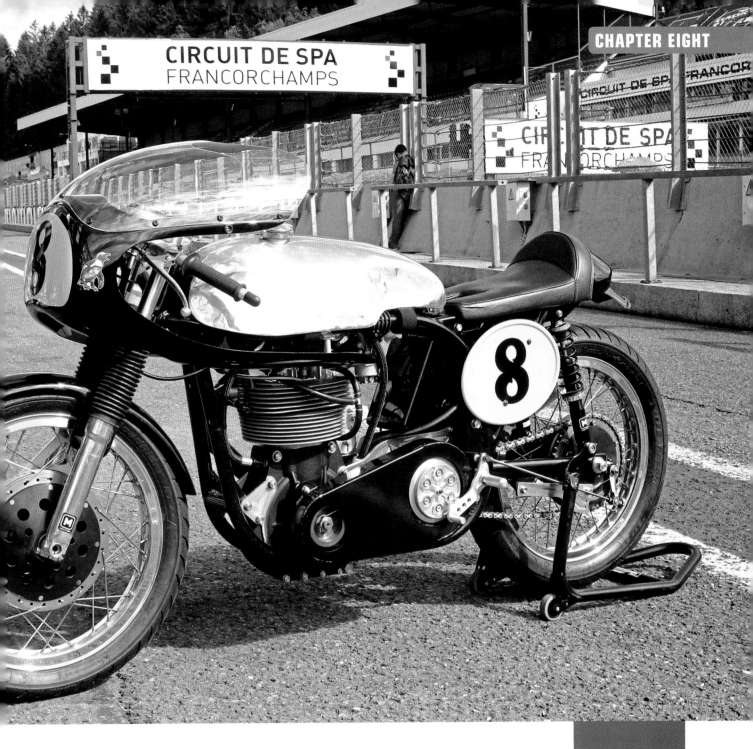

cylinder bores and a whole range of valve sizes – but all of these were secondary to reliability. In the adage which was prevalent at the time: "To finish first, first you have to finish…"

By the winter of 1960/61, Mike Hailwood's talent was recognised as something completely remarkable and so father Stan decided to hire Lacey, and his talented daughter Ann, to work exclusively on Norton engines for Ecurie Sportive – the Hailwood team. The aim would be to provide Mike with the very best 500cc grand prix engines in the world – clearly, after the factory four cylinder MV Agustas!

Not that the relationship between Hailwood senior and Lacey was an easy one. Stan was a self-made millionaire and master of all he surveyed. Lacey was acknowledged as a genius, and acolytes hung on his every word.

Neither was under endowed in the ego department and arguments between the two were frequent, culminating with Lacey storming out – and Hailwood having to carefully coax him back to the project.

The rest of the Ecurie Sportive bike was a lot more standard – for a top of the range, grand prix Norton. There wasn't anything better than the legendary Featherbed frame, and the Norton front forks and Girling rear shocks were state of the art. In practice, the Ecurie Sportive chassis was the best available.

The 8in (200mm) rear Manx hub was also as good as anything but the top GP runners of the day all used the 9in (230mm), twin leading shoe, Oldani front brake which was an order of magnitude better than every other stopper.

To make the best of the Lacey Norton engine, »

Our Ecurie Sportive Norton – a strong contender for the world's most beautiful race bike

a very, very expensive six-speed Schafleitner gearbox was fitted to the bike. The standard Norton clutch was retained along with its exposed primary chain which was lubricated by having oil dripped on it – ideal for getting on to the rear tyre!

As I finished telling the story to Patrick, I paused – and then really took the pin out of the hand grenade. "I wonder what Stan would have had for Mike if he had been building a Norton today?"

The "What if…" game had just been moved into the world of current classic bikes.

Now for another aside. Patrick Walker is a university educated, formally trained engineer with a passion for Manx Nortons. His bikes dominate the Lansdowne Classic Racing Series – the premier division of classic motorcycle racing. They are fast but pragmatically functional because this is how Patrick sees a racing motorcycle.

Despite being desperately competitive, Patrick

is also a purist. He won't have anything to do with fakes, in any form, and this is one of the many reasons I admire him. He is also a thoroughbred engineer – and this has its advantages and disadvantages.

For example, to Patrick, 1mm is one thousandth of a metre or 0.039 inches. It doesn't mean anything more or less than that.

To me, 1mm is a very small distance which is ever so tiny but not really as minute as a tappet clearance, which is really, really small but which is also bigger than lots of things, whose names I forget, but which are inside an engine and, for that matter, other parts of the bikes and which remind me of… you know, we had a tiny little insect in our paddock and the end of its proboscis was ever so wonderfully miniscule, much less than 1mm, and there it was feeding off the pollen on a plum flower – and how interesting is that? Yes, 1mm is a very useful adjective.

Much as I like and admire Patrick's bikes, I

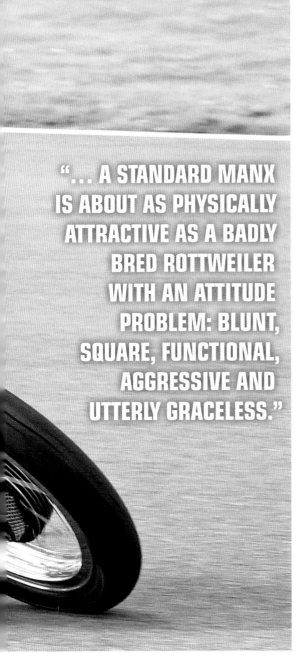

"... A STANDARD MANX IS ABOUT AS PHYSICALLY ATTRACTIVE AS A BADLY BRED ROTTWEILER WITH AN ATTITUDE PROBLEM: BLUNT, SQUARE, FUNCTIONAL, AGGRESSIVE AND UTTERLY GRACELESS."

Mike Hailwood with the original Ecurie Sportive Norton

have never wanted to own one. It's not that the bikes are anything but rocket ships, or that the engineering is not superb, but simply because a standard Manx is about as physically attractive as a badly bred rottweiler with an attitude problem – blunt, square, functional, aggressive and utterly graceless.

I am at the end of my racing life now and have long since given up being bothered about success – or lack of it. Now, I wanted a racing motorcycle which performed wonderfully but which was also catch-your-breath beautiful – a bike which compelled you to touch it, last thing at night, for the sheer tactile joy of being so close to beauty. I was chasing the ephemeral and subtle, and these are not easy targets.

The final part of the story is that I have spent all my working life as a journalist, criticising and commenting on the designs of others. In the real world of real motorcycles and real money, could I do any better?

So, Patrick and I agreed a price which was

vastly more than I could afford, or justify, and vastly less than the cost of the bike, because we both wanted to make not a copy or fake of the 1961 Ecurie Sportive bike but a homage to it – the "What if…" game in metal.

We laid the foundations of the project outside Patrick's van with the bike's colour. The original Ecurie Sportive Norton was white so our bike would be black – as far away as we could possibly get from making a fake anything.

After this momentous decision, things got much harder – for both of us.

The problem was not nearly as straightforward as it seems. Without resorting to any computer generated, virtual reality programmes I can see things with pellucid clarity, merely by half-closing my eyes and letting my mind do the rest. I can then describe what I have seen. So far, so good.

Unfortunately, what Patrick needed was a set of measurements and precise specifications and so the fun began. 》

In some ways, many ways in fact, the mechanical aspects of the bike were the easy part. The heart of the engine was one of Patrick's normal, two-valve, 86mm bore engines, the same basic specification as Bill Lacey was using for the Ecurie Sportive engines.

The big difference at the top end of the engine is that Patrick uses enclosed coil valve springs, instead of the exposed hair pin springs of the Lacey bike which allowed oil to spray everywhere. Things were not so environmentally sensitive in 1960!

In the spirit of the great W G Lacey himself, Patrick wanted to try some new, pre-prototype valve gear parts that he had designed just for the Ecurie Sportive motor. Being highly experimental, Patrick wanted feedback from me as part of his continuous improvement strategy. Only when they were proven in the ES engine would they be put on sale. Truly, I would be a works, 'Works Racing', rider again!

The cylinder barrel is Nikasil coated. This is a mixture of silicone and carbide, electro-plated directly on to the aluminium of the barrel. The finish permits extremely good heat transfer and is porous, so retaining lubricant. When a Nikasil coated barrel is honed correctly, unbelievably tight piston clearances are possible. Patrick's pistons are no more than five microns from perfect, over a bore of 86mm – whereas Lacey was lucky to find a barrel within 20 times of that tolerance. This is what modern engineering can achieve in practical terms.

Externally the bottom half of the engine looks identical to a Manx, unless you are a real expert on these engines, but is vastly different internally with a one piece, plain bearing crankshaft built to aerospace tolerances, and a modern oil pump circulating thin, fully synthetic Silkolene 15-50w race oil.

In fact, the engine has everything which Bill Lacey would have put into the Hailwood bike 56 years ago.

The gearbox is a six-speeder, just like Mike's, but although the external castings look similar to a 1960's Norton, internally the Mick Hemmings' produced box is pure 21st century with a smooth, silent change which would grace any 2016 bike. Only the original right-hand shift, with up for first gear and down for the

Patrick Walker did a brilliant job interpreting my ideas for a beautiful race bike

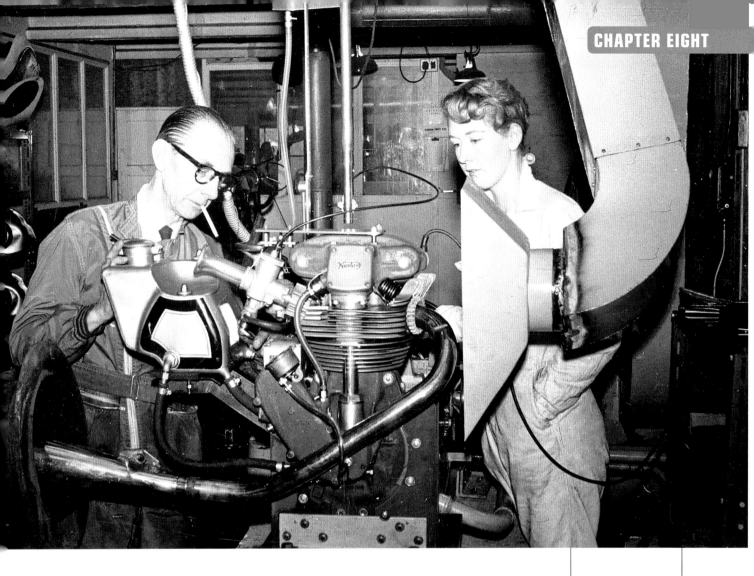

next five ratios, would have been recognised by Hailwood.

Imagining what Mike would have made of the belt drive is interesting. Instead of a fragile primary chain, lubed by oil drips, the ES has a toothed belt drive which runs perfectly clean, without any lubrication, and also acts as a shock absorber. The dry clutch, machined from billet alloy, is a masterpiece of British engineering produced by NEB in Coventry and really ought to be in a picture frame rather than being used for the vulgar job of controlling the bike's power.

The big difference between the Ecurie Sportive homage and Nortons from the 1950s and 1960s is the quality of the engineering. Nowhere is this more obvious than in the iconic Featherbed frame. Lacey's determinedly selective engineering ensured that Mike's bike was as near to perfect as the manufacturing practices of the day permitted but every single frame which Patrick has made is precisely to specification, using Norton's original Bracebridge Street drawings – and on a frame jig which is true and accurate. The chassis of our homage bike would have brought a smile to Lacey's face.

Where the smile would have changed to admiration is with the suspension. Just a couple of miles from our house is Maxton Engineering which makes some of the best suspension in

the modern world. Additionally, the team there produces the cleverest classic racing suspension anywhere in the galaxy!

Technically, I wanted Maxton suspension on the bike but Ron, Mary and Richard – who own and run Maxton – brought something else to the project, a wonderful mixture of enthusiasm, kindness and care. These are ephemeral traits but manifest themselves in a very real way for a project like this one.

At the rear was a pair of gas pressurised shocks which, unlike the Girlings which Mike Hailwood used, actually function perfectly throughout their range of travel. The front Norton forks were completely reworked with precision shims which provide sensitivity and feel equal to the best 2016 fork.

So now we had all the important bits of the bike except for one, its appearance. I wanted a long, elegant, ellipse of a motorcycle which looked as if it was doing 100mph on its paddock stand, so I specified a tiny, near anorexic, bikini fairing which flowed across the bike like a wraith of mist.

In response Patrick fitted a great big, fat blob of carbon fibre which was designed to provide excellent high-speed protection at the TT. This was the correct technical solution but was a million miles away from what I wanted »

Bill Lacey and daughter Ann working on the Ecurie Sportive engine which brought Mike Senior TT success.
Image: Mortons Archive

aesthetically. And so the discussions went on, and on, and on…

Probably, the best way of describing the outcome was that Patrick won 95% of the engineering debates and I got my wishes with the majority of the styling.

And how Patrick worked to put my ideas into practice. Take the black on the bike. Black is virtually unknown in modern painting because it always has an addendum so that it becomes black with a hint of brown, blue, metallic or something. By contrast, on our bike the black is base black, hand applied and rubbed and rerubbed until it has such depth that you can swim in it. This black is point zero on the black scale!

The exhaust, fabricated entirely from titanium, arcs across the bike like a python on the hunt and, after a long debate, concludes in an elegant, tapered silencer which is pure motorcycle art.

As I bombarded him with emails, Patrick toiled with the detail which makes the bike special.

Titanium is everywhere and the engine plates are milled to save a gnat's bacon bap of weight. Not only are they milled but Patrick wrote the CNC computer programme so that there are the merest hints of tool marks arcing to and fro across the metal, in a modern tribute to the engine turning of old.

And then there is the petrol tank, a hand-made, graceful series of infinite curves which makes a standard Manx tank look like a five gallon jerry can from a pound shop. Patrick apologised that the workings of the English Wheel and planishing hammer could still be seen on the tank and offered to get it sprayed in silver to the same standard as the rest of the bike, and I almost wept in despair!

So the tank stays as naked as the day it was born, bearing testimony to its creator's skill with hand tools and the eye of a genius. Truly, deep in the English Midlands, metal working magic still exists.

The final result is a 500cc motorcycle weighing in at 275lb (125kg) with looks which stop admirers in their tracks.

And, of course, the end of the fairy tale should be that the aging hero rode off into the distance on his perfect steed – except that he didn't. The first test session was a disaster. Nothing fitted me. My new, hand-made, bespoke English suit hung off me like cheap hire clothes at a chav's wedding.

Patrick toiled with a smile which would have done credit to any saint and we finally got everything in precisely the right places for me: then the troubles really began.

The bike wouldn't steer, or stop and so, instead of coming home with us, back it went

The ES Norton is supermodel slim

to Patrick for some serious TLC. The brake was easily sorted with some simple corrective machining which the Italian manufacturer of the Oldani front brake should have done from the start.

The suspension was a much bigger task. The problem was that there are myriad combinations of fork spring lengths and weights for every Manx and so each bike is effectively a one-off job.

The Maxton team was supremely helpful, not to say kind, but it wasn't a two minute fix to get the suspension to precisely match the bike – and me. Don't ever think that building a one-off bike which is intended to be raced, as distinct from just being a show object, is easy.

So, there we are with the sun shining and the ES bike outside our designated garage at the fabulous Spa circuit and along comes a serious collector of MV Agusta GP machines. He spends 10 minutes examining our Norton from every angle and then says: "You have the most beautiful bike at Spa." At that compliment, I almost choked with emotion.

But the looks were not the reason for building the bike. On what is the best racetrack in the world, my dream, which Patrick made live, was flawless. The motor

pulled hard and revved like a 125 GP bike and all the days of work which Maxton put into the suspension produced the best handling classic race bike I have ever ridden.

Dropping down past the old pits and heading towards the legendary Eau Rouge, our tribute to Hailwood's Ecurie Sportive team was singing. With my head buried in the wonderful alloy fuel tank, I had a long look ahead and pondered whether I could take the chicane with 7000rpm on the tach in fifth gear – 100mph plus and a real achievement for a fat, bald, old, wrinkly racer. And I could! At that point, I declared the project a total success.

The relationship between a rider and a race bike is difficult to articulate but, at its best, there is an intense, anthropomorphic intimacy. Our bike has these traits in every way so that I become part of the bike, and the motorcycle an extension of me. And, as we passed modern GP bikes one after another, the effort, the money and the frustration of the last 14 months disappeared.

I was riding the most sublimely beautiful race bike in the world and one which performed as well as it looked – and it was coming home with me. How lucky can one person be? ∎

The fabulous Norton Manx grand prix motor but now with hand-made titanium exhaust

POSTSCRIPT:

I was initially reluctant to include this addendum to the story but I have now heard it from two impeccable sources both of whom came, separately, to admire our homage to the Ecurie Sportive Norton. Neither knew that the other person had told it to me so who knows, it might even be true.

Lacey delivered his super Manx engine late for the TT but, with Hailwood in the saddle, it proved to be a flyer. Mike won the Senior TT, for 500cc machines, at an average of 100.61 mph which was astonishingly fast. In second and third places respectively were Bob McIntyre and Tom Phillis, two of the finest riders in the world.

Unfortunately, Hailwood senior and Lacey allegedly had yet another enormous fall out after the race so Mr Lacey removed the engine from the ES Norton and took it back to Brooklands where, and this is the high drama part of the whole saga, he dug a hole and buried it – swearing that no one else would ever use his masterpiece.

So, if you have a metal detector, and a lot of patience, perhaps there is a legendary piece of British racing history somewhere beneath the Brooklands' soil.

Let me know when you find it….

KNOX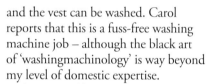

KNOX TRACK VEST

I have been using the Knox Track Vest for several years now and, like a lot of products from this Cumbrian firm, I still wonder why someone hadn't invented this piece of riding gear years ago.

First, why bother with back protection? After a rider's head, the most vulnerable part of the body is the spine. Just writing about the subject stresses me but the bottom line is that a back protector ought to be standard wear every single time you take out a bike. I'm no angel in this respect, and I still love riding in a t-shirt and shorts on a perfect summer's day but, equally, I know that that a triple whammy burger, obviously with extra fries, followed by ice cream and a chocolate topping, is not a smart way to eat in the long term. It's a matter of knowing the risk and then deciding to take it – or not. Generally speaking, back protectors should be very high on the list of essential riding gear.

So why did Knox introduce the Track Vest? For road riders, the answer is that the vest can be worn under a textile jacket and so raise the standard of back protection to racing levels.

The vest's use for racing is rather more subtle. Ironically the better leathers fit, the more a separate back protector is a nuisance. A back protector needs to be accurately placed so that it protects as much of the rider's spine as possible, and I can't remember how many times I would wriggle my previous back protector into the correct place only to have the thing move as I zipped up my leathers.

The problem is exacerbated because Carol is there warming up the bike, and giving me the: "Get a move on – can't you see your race is going to the collecting box?" eye and I can't get my leathers off again to move the protector to where it should be – and all of this is not a good place to be, mentally, just five minutes before a race.

The Track Vest solves all of these problems in one complete fix. After the initial 10 minutes of moving the Velcro adjusters around so that the fit is perfect, I have not needed to alter the adjustment. It's simply a matter of closing the zip in the certain knowledge that everything will remain perfectly in place.

The actual protector is Knox's Aegis Level Two (EN1621-2:2014) and is as good as back protectors come in terms of safety. The Aegis is made up of small, hard, plastic rectangles which move freely in every direction. These sit on a padded foam backing.

I don't know whether Knox intended this to happen, but the Aegis appears to have a memory. In use, a new protector always feels slightly odd until it learns the shape of your body. After this, it completely disappears from the consciousness.

In this case, the back protector zips into the vest body, with top quality YKK zips, so that it can be removed

and the vest can be washed. Carol reports that this is a fuss-free washing machine job – although the black art of 'washingmachinology' is way beyond my level of domestic expertise.

The vest itself is constructed of the new, British made, wonder fabric Meryl Lycra which is claimed to have unequalled wicking qualities. I don't know how this is established but certainly the Track Vest is wonderfully comfortable in use.

At the front is some very nominal padding – better than nothing but only just.

The cut is absolutely on the money with generous cutaways for the arms. Once more, in use it is impossible to know that one is wearing the Track Vest. The vest comes in a wide range of sizes all the way from small to XXL – which is seriously generously proportioned.

Finally, I am pleased to say that the Track Vest is made in England, actually not too far from my old sponsor at Crooks Suzuki, so there are no doubts about the quality.

CHAPTER NINE

KNOX COVERT WATERPROOF SPORT GLOVES

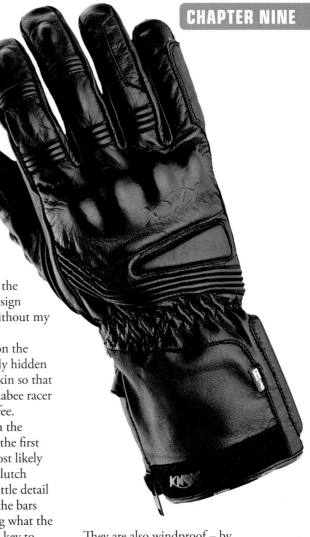

Racing motorcycles is a huge help in terms of road riding, not the least because racers tend to have a much greater feel for surfaces than their touring companions. The problem is that we are also ever so fussy and nit picking over riding clothing, and never more so than with gloves.

Try as I might, and I really have tried, I cannot manage to ride in thick, clumsy road gloves. You know the handlebars should be providing a strong sensation of what the front wheel is doing but the feeling simply isn't there.

This is why I have always insisted on riding in thin racing gloves in conditions which were patently too cold and too wet to be sensible. At one time, I simply suffered but then heated grips came along and so I still suffered – but a little less.

Then, along came the Knox Covert glove and things changed forever.

Like many Knox products, the Covert glove is a complex piece of kit. It is made from 25% goat leather, 70% cow skin and 5% nylon.

Bonded to the inside of the glove is Knox's own Outdry patented waterproof membrane. This is hugely better, and I really can't overstate the importance, than conventional waterproof membranes which move about inside the glove.

The palm is curved, although not as much as a full-on race glove, and there is the Knox scaphoid protection. These super hard, and very slippery little pads, really do work.

I slid off at Donington a few years ago and, when I came to a halt, the scaphoid pad was worn to nothing but my wrist was fine. My wallet was severely mangled paying for the damage, but at least I could sign the cheque for the repairs without my hand hurting!

There is more protection on the knuckles but Knox has subtly hidden this beneath a layer of goatskin so that one doesn't look like a wannabee racer arriving at the café for a coffee.

There are anti-slip areas on the palms and on the insides of the first two fingertips – the ones most likely to be used for braking and clutch control. Once more, these little detail touches increase the feel to the bars and so to the tyres. Knowing what the tyres are doing is the golden key to riding safely.

Continuing with the touring theme, the glove is closed via a zip and has an opening which is amply wide enough to allow a riding jacket beneath it or it can be fully closed and the cuff worn externally if you prefer.

Overall, the glove oozes quality with little embroidered tags and micro badges showing that someone at Knox really cares about the product. Embroidery and badges don't improve the quality of the glove but they do show passion, and I really like this.

So how do the gloves work in practice?

First, the Covert gloves are a compromise, so don't expect the intense, membrane thin feel of a race glove. Equally, the feel through the bars will let you know what is happening in a way which no conventional touring glove ever does.

They are also windproof – by summer riding terms. Riding in English summer temperatures of between 18°C and 22°C, as I have done, they have been perfect.

The Covert gloves are surprisingly waterproof. I try to avoid recreational rain riding these days but I did get caught out in some serious rain and it was two hours before I powerboated into our drive – still with dry hands!

I have banged on at length about their suitability for racing and sports use but their discreet appearance would make them ideal for fashion conscious classic riders who want a traditional looking glove but with modern protection.

There is a range of sizes from small to XXL. The sizing really does cover a wide range of hand shapes so you will be able to find a glove which will fit you accurately.

At £99, the Covert gloves aren't cheap but they are outstandingly good value and, even if they hadn't been supplied free of charge for me to test, I would have happily spent my own money on them.

To conclude, these are the gloves I have been seeking for the last 40 years and I love them! ■

> **"THESE TOUCHES INCREASE THE FEEL TO THE BARS AND SO TO THE TYRES. KNOWING WHAT THE TYRES ARE DOING IS THE GOLDEN KEY TO RIDING SAFELY."**

Looking a bit desperate as I screw the thingys off the wonderful little Kawasaki

MOTORCYCLING LIFE

L'ENDURO DES SABLES

Or – Où est le premier virage s'il vous plaît?

Finishing 135th in a race is something which would not, normally at least, be a source of pride but rather a subject I would go a mile to avoid. But, the L'Enduro des Sables in 1978 was the exception.

I rode my man bits off, took immense life threatening risks and, with the huge slice of luck which clubman racers need if they are ever to achieve anything, finished well inside the top 10% at Le Touquet. I also didn't get killed, which was very nice – in every way, a memorable double success! »

Desperate work in the parc fermé. The little KE175 was amazing to keep going with the stick I gave it

On occasions, I do wonder whether I should have paid more attention in Miss Pillar's French lessons instead of spending my time surreptitiously reading *MCN*. The 1978 Le Touquet Beach Race, where I came close to being killed on several occasions, was one of them.

The story begins in August 1977. The weather at the Belgian round of the 500cc World Motocross Championship was blistering and, inside the Citadel of Namur, the dust had hovered like dense clouds of light brown talcum powder for the whole of practice.

Whatever you thought of GP motocross riders in the 1970s, no one could doubt their courage. Truly, they had cojones like fit Hereford bulls but on that August Sunday, they just refused to ride – so dangerous were the conditions.

The track at Namur threaded its way, one bike wide, through the trees and around the houses and visibility was

zero. Someone was going to get killed so there was a wholly justifiable strike.

I was working as journalist and photographer and to fill the time until the GP was on again I gossiped to a French journalist. Ahhh, Miss Pillar was sitting in heaven smiting me for my inattention in her classes.

The Gallic journo explained that every January, there was a light-hearted mess about at Le Touquet where a few of the off-road boys got together for a sort of track day on the beach, glugged a lot of wine and ate some rather fine food. At the time, I was pretty handy as an enduro rider and there was nothing much happening in Britain in January, so why not have a trip over La Manche, show off with a few power slides on the beach and then get stuck into le menu gastronomique? At least, this is what I thought I had translated.

The first problem was that, at the time, I was riding a Suzuki for Eddie Crooks, my 1977 bike had been sold and the 1978 model had yet to arrive. Still, with Ed's permission, I

> ## "SO, WITH A BIT OF FAIRLY POLITE ELBOWING AND CONVENIENT MISUNDERSTANDING OF INSTRUCTIONS, I SOON MANOEUVRED THE KWACK TO THE FIRST ROW."

The overnight parc fermé for the 1500 competitors in L'Enduro des Sables

was allowed to ask Arthur Arnold, the owner of Knott Mill Motorcycles in Manchester, if I could borrow his Kawasaki KE 175 trail bike demonstrator.

It is important to put the baby Kwack into perspective. The bike was an utterly non-competition spec road biased trailie, aimed at commuting and light recreational use. However, there were a smattering of these little motorcycles being used in club enduros and they had gained a reputation for being bombproof reliable, not to say surprisingly competent off-road.

I explained to Arthur that Le Touquet was a bit of light-hearted fun but he was

concerned. What if it wasn't such a play event as I thought? What if it was actually a race? I dismissed his worries but Arthur still insisted on putting a break resistant, enduro lights kit on the bike and a set of race knobblies.

So now we had a cute little street trail bike which looked as if it might manage some light off-road riding. How cool would that be when I was doing my demo donuts?

The first hint of suspicion came when I received what looked awfully like race entry forms. The man behind L'Enduro des Sables was Thierry Sabine – the mastermind of the Paris-Dakar races – and at this point I should not so much have smelled a rat but a » whole flock of malodorous rodents. Thierry never, ever did easy.

Still, what could go wrong? If it was a bit of a race, so what? I was riding nationals, and the occasional international enduro, so no problemo.

Sometimes racers just can't take a hint. Have you ever seen a cross channel ferry rocking violently – when it is tied up to the quay in Dover Harbour?

Still, we had got a brilliant deal on the trip to Boulogne and the English Channel isn't like a proper sea is it? If it wasn't a real sea, the masses of green water breaking over the upper deck lounge window gave a good imitation of the perfect storm. I was sick, my go-for was sick, the ship's crew were sick and, I guess that down below, the little Kawasaki threw up too.

We staggered off at Boulogne and I had to almost immediately stop the van – to be sick again. Thank goodness I wasn't riding in a serious race the following day.

Ten miles out from Le Touquet the rats started to need deodorant again. The roads were absolutely jammed with bikes large and small. Full-on enduro bikes screamed past on the grass verges, mopeds pushed through on either side whenever we stopped and passengers in Wehrmacht replica BMW sidecar outfits swung their machine guns round on the cheering crowds. This didn't feel at all right.

Scrutineering confirmed my worst nightmares. This was a race, and a proper one too. We unloaded the little Kwack and joined the end of the queue. An hour later, a

snowdrop appeared. It blossomed and died. The queue moved again. Continents were formed quicker than our progress towards the scrutineering team.

What made things worse was everything which obsessed British scrutineers held no interest for the French. Brakes: don't care. Self-closing throttle: it's up to you. Race numbers: oui, parfait. But the lights – goodness me, the lights! Did they work? Being a road bike they actually functioned quite well. Now main beam, now dip, now main beam again. I was beginning to think that this was a night race.

Cold, tired and feeling as if I had just spent three hours throwing up on a channel ferry, I slunk off to the hotel.

The mussels in white wine, garlic and parsley looked delicious. And indeed, they proved

to be so – until the first one hit my stomach and it was off to les toilettes again.

It was a long night and an interesting one. I lay on the bed, doubled up in agony while, outside the hotel, the final of the all France unsilenced moped race was in full swing. As the last mopeders exited at 5am I crashed into a tortured sleep until the alarm went off 20 minutes later.

One look at the croissants convinced me that food was not a good option so we set off to retrieve the little Kwack and discover what the day held.

The first problem was that the bike and the work areas lay a couple of miles apart and only I could, or more accurately would, drive in the mayhem. Still, with much "Allez! Allez! Je suis un pilote!" we forced the borrowed Tranny »

This picture is from a later race but it gives a good idea of the conditions I faced — until I started slipstreaming Yamaha works rider Serge Bacou

van to the seafront and what a shock. Next to us was the factory SWM team which had travelled all the way from Italy. Spare wheels, quick filler fuel cans, three factory mechanics and a team manager. I looked at our single jerrycan of pump fuel, one tin of chain lube and the Kwack's tool roll and the smelly rat inside my head beamed the smile of the knowing. Truly, Mr Cock Up had come for le petit déjeuner!

The first problem was to recover the bike from the parc fermé outside the town hall. This was not as difficult as it seems. I had paid a little bit of attention to Miss Pillar so it was merely a case of standing in the middle of a stream of traffic doing 60mph, flagging down the first bike to make eye contact and demanding a lift to the town hall. Simple if you have no sense of danger and you're desperate!

When I arrived there it was like the Challenge Cup Final at Wembley, half an hour before kick-off. Bikes were everywhere and a dense fog of two-stroke fumes hung over the parc fermé as riders battled with their bikes, arm waving officials, increasingly tense police dogs and each other for a slot through the one bike wide exit gate.

Once out into Le Touquet's elegant town centre, things became even worse. You've never seen true danger until an amateur tries to pull his first ever wheelie surrounded by 1000 over hyped racers and then crashes into a lamppost, bringing down five of his fellow competitors.

Girlfriends rush out to plant kisses on the cheeks of their heroes, grandad is wheeled out into the centre of the road to shake his son's hand and mum stuffs a baguette sandwich down the riding jacket of her little boy. The amateur racer's life revealed in living colour.

By this time, I was feeling fine. The threat of real, serious danger and a lot of racing experience had combined to kick in the adrenaline and focus my mind. This job had the potential to get me killed.

The chaos was even worse at the start. I never did find out the number of starters but it lay between 1200 and 1500 and the idea was that there would be three rows of 500 or so – and that's a lot of bikes – arranged on the beach with the quickest riders seeded to row one.

I was directed to the third row and I could immediately see the problem of hurtling down the beach with 1000 bikes in front of me. So, with a bit of fairly polite elbowing and convenient misunderstanding of instructions, I soon manoeuvred the Kwack to the first row. **»**

Directly in front of us was a water-filled ditch which stretched the whole width of the beach and into the sea. In fact, at the far right 50 or 60 riders were actually in the water. In front, stretching out of sight, was flat empty sand.

I hadn't a clue where the course lay so I asked the KTM rider next to me how far it was to the first corner. He smiled and said: "Huit kilomètres sur la gauche."

Eight kilometres – that was five miles and flat out all the way. Suddenly, the cross channel sea-sickness returned.

We were told to watch a Land Rover parked in the water and when someone waved something the race would start. It didn't happen like that. The waves started breaking over the bikes in the sea and, with the wholly reasonable excuse that they were drowning, off they went and L'Enduro des Sables started.

For the first 25 yards, the Kwack was competitive and I was in the leading group. Then we weren't!

I simply pinned the throttle, lay flat on the tank road racing style, and prayed. Why the sudden affection for God? All around were

high speed crashes as riders with more bike than ability discovered that riding at 90mph on wet sand demands a considerable degree of skill.

In front of me, a tricked out Yamaha XT500 started to weave. The golden rule in these situations is to sit back on the saddle and nail the throttle. The Yam's pilot shut off and leaned forward.

It's a fascinating sight to see a rider cartwheel through the air in front of you but not nearly so interesting as observing a white fuel tank, gushing petrol, bounce down the track directly at your bike.

The tank is travelling at 60mph up the beach and I am travelling at 60mph down the beach. This is going to hurt. I tuck my left shoulder tight into the Kwack and petrol sprays from the Yam's tank as it neatly pirouettes over my shoulder. It was that close.

The first corner is a motorcycling version of the Charge of the Light Brigade. Bikes are everywhere – on their sides, upside down, on fire, bent, broken and no longer of this world.

I came down two gears and blasted through, round and, yes I have to admit it, over bikes

My good friend and sponsor, Colin Shutt, loaned me his van for the event and Arthur Arnold provided the KE175. It was good to have mates who liked racing

and riders. Even so, it was surprising how long you can hear the scream of someone who has just had a knobbly tyre spin over his private parts!

The rest of the 15 mile course was very natural and simply ran up one giant sand dune and down the other. Chaos ruled but the baby Kwack ran to perfection – all the way up to within half a mile from the service area. Then it started to cut out. I flicked the fuel tap on to reserve in case sand had got into the tank and pressed on. Clearly, the bike wouldn't do another lap like this with sand in the tank so I pulled in for a check. The answer was obvious. There was no fuel.

Normally, the KE175 would do a comfortable 40mpg even off-road. At Le Touquet, I was caning the bike so hard that this had fallen to 10mpg.

Lap two showed that sometimes the god of racing loves amateurs. The blast down the beach was as bad as ever but the first corner was 10 times worse and the hills were blocked solid with the dead bikes and nearly dead riders. Then the sun came out.

Factory Yamaha rider Serge Bacou came blasting past and as he reached the base of the first killer hill an army of hitmen from Sonauto,

the French Yamaha importer, appeared. Two grabbed the fork legs on Serge's bike and another four ran in front and hurled bikes and bodies out of the way. I stayed glued to the rear wheel of the Yam and suddenly I was rising up the race order – and rapidly too. It must have been the slowest ever slipstreaming but it was effective.

In between hills I rode with reckless determination to keep Bacou in sight and it worked. Another hill and a further 100 up the order.

On the final lap, I actually waited to be lapped by another factory Yamaha rider and off we went again.

I did three laps without getting killed, which I count as one of my best ever rides, but I wasn't looking forward to the second leg to be held after lunch. I need not have worried. The gale force winds drove the tide up the beach and even the French had to abandon the job.

So, I can claim, I think, to be the first Englishman ever to compete in L'Enduro des Sables and, with 135th place from an entry of over 1500, probably the happiest too – thanks of course to becoming an unofficial member of the Works Yamaha team – and while riding a Kawasaki! ■

Honda CB 400 – Honda got form and function absolutely right with this iconic motorcycle

HONDA CB400F1

ONE OF HONDA'S GREATEST MOTORCYCLES

I never actually owned a Honda CB400 but I did ride a lot of them when they were the default sports bike in Britain. The only reason for not actually spending my own money on one was that I was a bit tall and heavy to get the best out of a 400.

In terms of outright anything – speed, handling, braking, specification – nothing on the CB400 was outstanding, but the whole package was. Maybe best of all was that you could ride the 400 flat out everywhere, all the time, and you'd never be able to break it. For naughty boys in the 1970s this is why the bike remains their fondest memory.

"IN ESSENCE, THE 350 '4' WAS JUST TOO WELL-BEHAVED A MOTORCYCLE. IT BRUSHED ITS TEETH EVERY MORNING, COMBED ITS IMMACULATE HAIR, ALWAYS WORE CLEAN JEANS WHICH WERE FRESHLY IRONED AND ONLY DRANK ONE CAN OF BEER ON A SATURDAY EVENING."

The CB 400 engine was completely indestructible... absolutely unbreakable

have been riding motorcycles for a long time and, fortunately, I have not lost any of my passion for bikes. I have ridden an awful lot of good bikes, a few mediocre ones and the occasional two-wheeled horror story but a few, rather special motorcycles, are truly memorable.

One of these is the Honda CB400F1 which simply makes me smile with the memory of riding one of the nicest motorcycles ever to grace a highway.

The CB400 isn't perfect but it is such a thoroughly good motorcycle that even its worst enemy would find it hard to say a word against it.

The CB400's dad was the technically brilliant, but rather dull, CB350. The CB350 was allegedly built at the behest of Soichiro Honda who felt that a 350cc motor was the perfect size for a four cylinder road bike. The problem

was that whilst 'Pops' Honda loved the 350, paying customers didn't. This is not surprising since the 350 '4' was slower, heavier, more expensive and cost more to build than its twin cylinder brother, the 325cc CB350 Dream.

In essence, the 350 '4' was just too well-behaved a motorcycle. It brushed its teeth every morning, combed its immaculate hair, always wore clean jeans which were freshly ironed and only drank one can of beer on a Saturday evening. As your bank manager it would have been fine. As a friend to party with, it was a disaster.

Honda's answer was elegantly simple. The 350 '4' was a fine motorcycle. It just needed some help to come out from behind the door and reveal its true potential.

The first job was to take the 350's power plant to the gym. Incredibly for such a sophisticated motor, it was under square at »

CB400s were incredibly competent race bikes. Here's Tony Rutter on the Mocheck Honda with its exhausts cut and tucked in — as I did to Colin Wilkinson's bike

47mm x 50mm. Honda bored the new motor to take a 51mm piston which gave a marginally over square engine with a capacity of 408cc. New, bigger valves than the 350 plus a stronger clutch were fitted, and a four-into-one, siamesed exhaust system which both increased torque and looked cool.

A sweet, close-ratio, six-speed gearbox meant that the motor could be kept on the boil and the delightful howl from the long, tapering silencer took us grands prix wannabees right back to the golden days of Honda Racing with Jim Redman and Mike Hailwood.

The end result of Honda's re-engineering was a bombproof engine which gave a very healthy 37bhp @ 10,000 rpm – equivalent to around

100mph with a small, light rider tucked in tight on the fuel tank. This needs putting into perspective. 37bhp was slightly more power than a good 350cc Aermacchi or AJS 7R produced, and these were still competitive in grands prix four years earlier.

The chassis remained more or less unchanged in terms of being small and light but, cosmetically, the new bike was very much a sports bike. The flat bars, narrow tank and seat and, most of all, an engine which positively demanded to be revved, all pointed to hard riding.

Honda encouraged the café racer image that the CB400 inculcated and this was both good and bad in terms of sales. The firm suspension

"...IT WAS NEVER GOING TO BEAT THE KILLER QUICK KAWASAKIS OF THE DAY BUT IT WAS AN INFINITELY MORE REFINED AND SOPHISTICATED MOTORCYCLE..."

and high revving engine did not endear the bike to American riders and the USA, even more so than now, was the critical market for Honda.

By contrast European riders, with road racing genes running through their bodies, loved the CB400. With the beautiful little power unit howling between 6000 rpm and the red line at 10,000-plus, the Honda was a true race bike for the street. Hammered through rough corners, the firm suspension was in its element and best of all, it flattered the rider, regardless of their ability.

Only the brakes were less than ideal but with four-stroke engine braking available this was not a problem in the real world.

The 400 '4' was never going to beat the killer quick Kawasakis of the day but it was an infinitely more refined and sophisticated motorcycle, and one which won the hearts of all who rode it.

Today, CB400s are still recognised as outstanding motorcycles and this is a problem for would-be owners. On one side of the coin the 400 is a mass produced motorcycle with no racing pedigree or exotic bloodline. It is, however, one of the nicest motorcycles ever built. The end result is that it will take a solid £5000 to own one of the best examples of these lovely little bikes... although considerably less will buy you a running, but unrestored example. ■

The CB400's styling was wonderfully austere. Brits in particular loved it

TGO
154R

DAVID LESLIE RACING

POSTSCRIPT:

I got to know the CB400 on a rather more personal, intimate level than I would have perhaps liked. At school, I was considered to be academic and so was never allowed near anything to do with engineering.

However, I had raced bikes from the first time I could afford an entry fee and had become reasonably proficient at gas welding simply because, in those far off days, bikes broke all the time and needed mending.

Colin Wilkinson was long-time friend of mine and was a good national class racer. He had campaigned a very fast Norton for many years but, even by his tolerant standards, was weary of it breaking. In August 1975 Colin purchased a brand-new CB400 road bike with the intention of riding it in the 500cc class of the Manx Grand Prix, held over the incredibly tough Isle of Man TT course.

He arrived at my house with the bike having covered about five miles from new and asked that I cut and re-profile the exhaust pipes so that they tucked tight against the frame. The little Honda sat there with its exhausts gleaming and I began to feel like the vet approaching the happy looking stallion which was about to have its life changed.

Fortunately, I got the cuts right and, doubly fortunately, none of the welds broke during the killer tough two weeks of the 'Manx'. I would never claim to be a master craftsman but when it came to welding but my work was always durable.

Colin made a few basic modifications to the Honda and raised the gearing slightly. These mods, plus Colin's riding ability, were enough to give an 88mph lap in the Manx, and that was with the frame, suspension and motor completely standard.

Colin used it again in the Manx the following year and then sponsored another rider who finished eighth in the Production TT. In between, the CB400 was used as a commuter bike and for recreational riding.

10,000 miles later, the Honda was sold – still running perfectly and, except for checking the valve clearances, with the motor completely untouched. That's why riders loved the CB400!

> CB 400 detail was superb. What else could a super sports road bike need?

HONDA DN-01

THE 'DO NOT OWN 1' HONDA

Sometimes the memory of a bike – good or bad – remains with me for a long time after the road test is over and the article has been published. The DN-01 is one of these machines – such an appallingly dreadful creation that the whole of the design team for this monstrosity needs punishing by being made to ride the abomination as their only means of transport... for ever. That'd teach them!

I am often asked to name the best bike I have ever ridden, and the question is difficult to answer because I have been blessed with testing so many great motorcycles. But as for the worst – that's always easy: the DN-01!

Batman futuristic or just the recipient of an ugly stick beating. The ugly vote won overwhelmingly

Although I first began riding bikes slightly after the end of the Battle of Hastings in 1066, I still retain a childlike enthusiasm for new toys. Yes, I might prefer to ride my Manx Norton rather than the latest Ducati superbike, but that doesn't mean that I don't delight in sophisticated ECUs, super sticky tyres and dramatically efficient modern brakes.

I have another confession to make. I am somewhat biased towards Honda products, having been in awe of Soichiro's creations since the first Honda '4' screamed past me at Oulton Park in the 1960s. For me, Honda has not only made some of the most iconic motorcycles of all time, but some of the best too.

So that's the hors d'oeuvres out of the way, now on to the main course.

Honda's DN-01 shows what happens when engineers and marketing staff are allowed to come before the riders who actually purchase the bike.

I am sure the Honda suits sat around polished tables in planning meetings, giving each other all the reasons why the DN-01 would sell like heavily chilled bottled water in the middle of Death Valley. What they didn't do was to invite a rider – motorcycle or scooter – to offer an opinion. Forget the techno-babble and marketing hype. Would you, as a purchaser, write a cheque out for £11,000 for a dull, uncomfortable, poorly handling and impractical scooter? You wouldn't? Then all you good nice people at Honda have just got yourselves a pile of rotting bull dung to sell.

Perhaps the clearest view on what was happening at Honda came via the promo video which Honda had on YouTube when the bike was launched. This beautiful art film showed a vampish 1950s lady luring her leather helmeted, and DN riding lover to break the mould of convention and ride off into the distance.

There was plenty of symbolism but a distinct lack of reasons proffered as to why you should buy a DN-01, unless you like girls who smoke and wear long, silky dresses. In short, even after spending a fortune on a promo film, Honda still couldn't find anything solid to say about the DN.

The first problem is identifying what the DN-01 is. It is a bit like a scooter and has strong hints of custom cruiser thrown in too... while cunningly managing to fail in both categories.

So, where to start? The 'scike', or 'booter', (scooter bike?) is powered by a de-tuned version of Honda's 680cc V-twin engine which drove the wholly admirable Deauville mid-range tourer at the time. In the Deauville, the motor makes a respectable 60hp and is actually a very pleasant ride if you are not in too much of a hurry.

For European legislation reasons, British DNs were sold with a sleep inducing 33bhp while American DNs had a whole 12hp more.

In the DN, the v-twin motor is transformed into a dull, characterless power plant which has strong overtones of a generator unit – really, it does. The marketing gurus might have thought that having a V-twin would result in a rush of cruiser riders to the DN-01 but they should have first visited any Harley meet and »

Cornering on the DN was more akin to helming a yacht than riding a motorcycle. Note what's happening to the running boards... as it did on every bend

"WOULD YOU, AS A PURCHASER, WRITE A CHEQUE FOR £11,000 FOR A DULL, UNCOMFORTABLE, POORLY HANDLING AND IMPRACTICAL SCOOTER?"

The best that can be said about the DN-01 is that somewhere deep in Japan the bike must have had a motorcycling mummy who loved it... maybe

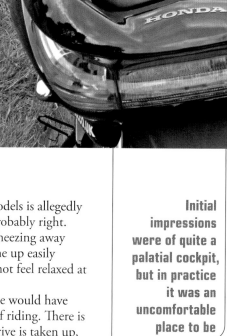

tried to get a real cruiser fan to exchange their Milwaukee twin for a DN-01. They would have been there a long time!

Now here is the part where the audience stands up at the Last Night of the Bike Proms, starts cheering and breaks out into a chorus of 'Bike of Hope and Glory'. Bolted on to the back of the Deauville engine is the smartest, smoothest automatic transmission ever to be seen on a bike.

It is a hydro-mechanical design in which the engine drives a hydraulic pump which then, ever so cleverly, controls a second pump through a swash plate. The second pump drives the rear wheel and the result is a seamlessly beautiful transmission of power from the engine to the rear wheel, via a shaft drive. Yes, it is a miracle of engineering neatness and yes, it does work in practice and yes, it is, very slightly, better than the automatic transmission found on scooters. So, well done Honda.

Now everyone is sitting down again, let's look at the real life experience. There are two drive modes 'D' and 'S'. The S option holds on to gears for longer and gives an allegedly more sporting performance. In practice, it makes almost no difference. In D, the DN-01 is as lethargic as a teenager being asked to mow the lawn on a Saturday morning. In S it is as lethargic as a teenager who has just been asked to mow the lawn on a Saturday afternoon. Mathematicians might discern the difference in reaction time, parents can't!

Press the left-hand side button to D and the transmission engages noiselessly. Open the throttle and there is a slight lag before the drive kicks in, and then you burble away like... well... like a rather de-tuned big scooter.

Once on the move, the transmission is perfect, which is good – but not that much better when compared with the standard setting Suzuki Burgman.

Top speed on European models is allegedly almost 100mph and this is probably right. With the generator engine wheezing away beneath my legs, 80mph came up easily enough but the 'booter' did not feel relaxed at these speeds.

It's also not all that the hype would have you believe in terms of ease of riding. There is a discernible lag before the drive is taken up, and the promises about ease of riding need questioning.

To all those newer riders, who might be fooled into believing that automatic transmission is a benefit, I would say stick at developing your riding skills and get the miles under your belt. A Kawasaki ER6, or Yamaha Fazer, is 10 times easier to ride in heavy traffic and is much more controllable, and therefore safer.

The DN also has a semi-auto mode but this is such an affectation that it is not worth mentioning. Yes, theoretically you can change gear semi automatically but the trouble is not worth the effort. Leave the DN in D and at least have the benefits of a scooter.

In fact, that's all the good news with the

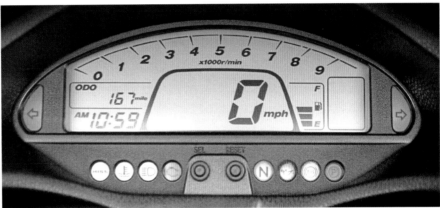

All that you need to enjoy the DN-01 is a very tight leotard, a funny hat and a suspiciously young friend called Robin

The instrument panel was very cutting edge technology and worked well. It's a pity it didn't have more of an influence on the rest of the bike

Inside there lives a super clever gearbox just trying to find the right place to do its job

DN-01, and from here things go rapidly downhill. First, the 'scike' is an uncomfortable thing to ride. I am 5ft 10in tall and this means that I was pushed back in the saddle so that the lip of the pillion cut into the small of my back. After 50 miles, I had really memorable backache.

The screen is utterly useless and managed to deflect the wind right into the space between my riding jacket collar and helmet, so with my head pinned back I was garrotted by the air at anything above 30mph. Now, riding down the PCH in California this might not be a problem but in cold and rainy Britain it most certainly is! Did Honda test this bike anywhere in the world with rain and temperatures below 20°C? I seriously doubt it.

At the same time, one's legs are forced forward in real cruiser style. If you rest your boots where they feel they should naturally go, the heel will drag through every corner with unfailing irritation.

Ah yes, corners. Riding a motorcycle through a corner is one of the great activities in life. It compares favourably to sipping a fine Chardonnay by the river on a warm summer evening or feeling the ski bite the snow as the turn is perfectly initiated.

Getting a corner perfectly right on a bike is a thing of beauty, of harmony, of sensory delight... an act which brings warmth to the soul, lightness to the heart and a smile to the rider's face. Corners are what make a bike a bike and not a car, tractor, lawnmower, truck or shopping trolley. Corners go straight to the heart and soul of a motorcycle.

»

Powering the DN was Honda's thoroughly charming Deauville engine – except Honda cut its man bits off

DN-01

HONDA
HFT

"...IT'S LIKE SENDING AN EMAIL TO THE CALLIPERS ASKING THEM TO GRIP THE DISCS WHEN THEY HAVE A SPARE MINUTE. HEAVEN HELP THE RIDER WHO HAS TO DO AN EMERGENCY STOP ON THE DN!"

Then there is cornering on a DN.

I prefer to use the words 'navigating a corner' when it comes to the DN, for the very good reason that being at the helm of a badly designed yacht and riding the DN are very similar activities. Because of its shallow head angle, the DN has to be forced to turn and then the forks flex and it wallows round with the rider giving a touch of rudder and then easing off again and then another tug at the rudder as the bend is negotiated. On a lake with a sailboat, this is dull and frustrating but the DN simply emasculates the joy of motorcycle riding, and that is unforgiveable.

Things don't get any better with the brakes. Potentially, the braking system is very clever. The rider squeezes a conventional brake lever on the right-hand side bar and this applies both brakes. With big discs – there is a 263mm disc at the front and triple pistons – the system should work very well, but it doesn't. Once again, it's the lack of rider involvement which is the problem. Brake and the bike does slow down, but it's like sending an email to the callipers asking them to grip the discs when they have a spare minute. Heaven help the rider who has to do an emergency stop on the DN!

Almost as an aside, you will note that there is no mention of using the rear brakes, for the very good reason that you will need legs the length of an adult giraffe to reach the pedal. Not that reaching it does any good because nothing much happens when the rear brake is applied.

If the DN is a thoroughly dispiriting experience then perhaps there are other reasons for putting one in your garage. To be honest, I quite like the swoopy Batman tribute looks and the DN is no more impractical than other cruisers. This is a bike to be seen on, rather than slaughtering 400 mountain road miles in a day. Unfortunately, like everything else about the bike – gearbox excepted – the DN misses the target by miles.

At one level, it is bling free... but what's a boulevard cruiser without mile deep paint and lustrous chrome? The DN has neither.

Honda insists that the DN is a practical motorcycle, like a Suzuki Burgman, so where are the heated grips and Sat Nav? In fact, where is anything to justify the £10,000 price ticket which someone at Honda optimistically stuck on the bike?

Now, the DN-01 has quietly slipped into oblivion to be replaced by much more sophisticated hybrids. Would you want one in your collection today? I really can't see a reason, unless you really do like quirky failures. Currently, very low mileage examples fetch around £4000 – but there are many better uses for your motorcycle collecting money. ∎

THE MUSCLE BIKE
KAWASAKI Z1

The Z1 is a bike I really wanted to own, as well as ride, but it came at a difficult time for me financially. I had just bought my first house and was setting up home with a new wife and, despite what the Millennials say today, things weren't any easier in 1973 – particularly from my social background!

Of course, racing, with its endless, voracious appetite for cash, didn't help either so I missed out on actually having a Z1 to call my own but I did ride a lot of these magnificent machines and they remain my favourite Japanese bike of the era.

The Honda CB750 was a bit too well-behaved and grown-up for me whereas the Z1 wasn't. In the early 1970s, if you wanted to go faster than a Z1 through the Welsh mountain roads which I love so much, then you needed to be flying a Hawk jet from RAF Valley. What an experience!

The Z1B is a big bike but in a muscular, rather than a podgy, way

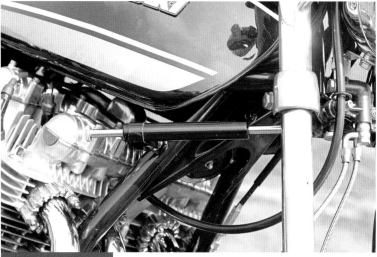

The big, 903cc four-cylinder engine was probably the best engineered power plant of its generation

It's time to correct one of the popular myths which is becoming ever more prevalent in the motorcycling world. Thus: "When Honda launched its 750 '4' in 1968, the biking world fell on its knees and worshipped the new arrival."

Those of us who were there at the time know this not to be the case. What Honda did was extremely, subtly clever. Just as the German blitzkrieg in the Second World War solved the problem of the supposedly impregnable French Maginot defensive line simply by going round the back of it, so Honda avoided the problem of selling a heavy, fairly dull, conservatively styled, four-cylinder motorcycle to hard-core bike enthusiasts by ignoring them.

If the leather-clad, oil-stained grand prix enthusiasts didn't want to buy the bike then the Idaho potato farmer, who learned everything he knew about motorcycles from his first and only experience with a Honda Dream, certainly did.

Honda produced a smooth, stone axe reliable street bike with an electric start which was maintenance free and never leaked a drop of oil – ever!

This was life with a Honda '4': Go to garage. Open door. Wheel Honda on to driveway. Insert key. Start. Ride. Park in garage.

Rider input was restricted to occasionally putting fuel in the tank. This was the new market which Honda recognised: two-wheeled car drivers.

By contrast, we hard-core motorcyclists

Yes, that's a steering damper and yes, you really, really, really did need it if you had any intention of riding the Z1 hard

thought that the Honda was a boring, old fashioned (even at launch) lump which held no attraction. What we wanted was a BSA Rocket 3 with its spine-tingling exhaust note and sublime handling. Except that in reality we didn't. We knew that the BSA would self-destruct before the Honda needed its second tank of petrol. Lusting after a triple was the norm. Writing a cheque out for one wasn't.

Despite Paul Smart's legendary win at Imola, only a fully paid-up member of the biking masochist's club would want to ride a 1972 Ducati Desmo. Appalling electrics, paint applied by a blind baboon with a migraine and haemorrhoid inducing vibration meant that Ducati's iconic V-twin was never going to be a mass market product.

What we wanted was a Honda '4' with biking sex appeal. We wanted a bike which was fast and reliable but we also wanted a motorcycle which induced lust. We wanted a bike which demanded to be stroked as the last thing before we went to sleep at night – a motorcycle which we had to caress before we left for work in the morning. We wanted a Kawasaki Z1.

In fact, the big Kwack was born twice. The first Kawasaki '4' was running and, almost, ready for launch in October 1968. This was good news and bad news for Kawasaki. The bad news was that Honda revealed its 750cc '4' at the Tokyo Show of that year. The good news was that Kawasaki scrapped its conservatively conceived four-cylinder machine and declared all-out war on its Japanese competitor.

The T103, as the bike was known internally in Kawasaki, was given top priority. The best of the Meguro engineers, the Japanese motorcycle company taken over by Kawasaki, were drafted in along with the Kawasaki staff who had done so well with the two-stroke triples.

A lot of consumer research was done, primarily in America, to confirm that there was indeed a market for a high performance four and then, in the spring of 1971, the first prototype was shipped to America for what has become a legendary test programme.

In America, T103 became 'Project New York Steak'. Led by Kawasaki America's senior test rider Bryon Farnsworth, and assisted by Kawasaki's race team of Gary Nixon, Hurley Wilvert and Paul Smart, the new Kawasaki was subjected to repeated attempts to break it.

One item on the test programme was undertaken at the Talladega Speed Bowl. The idea was to run the big Kwack flat out for the capacity of the fuel tank: quite literally nailed hard against the stop.

> **The forks and twin discs were a bit on the marginal side when it came to riding a Z1 hard – but who cared when the big Kwack would run up to 100mph in a blink**

Test riders reported weaving but, even when running at a genuine 130mph plus, the bike was unbreakable.

On normal roads, the T103 was run 8000 miles from LA to Daytona and back, this time thinly disguised as a Honda '4'. Drive chains lasted only 3000 miles and tyres only twice this distance but the all-new engine was bombproof.

Despite the encouragement from its test riders, Kawasaki was still nervous about the potential success of its new flagship and so »

"FIRST AND FOREMOST IT WAS, AND IS, UTTERLY, LUST INDUCINGLY GORGEOUS. THE FIT AND FINISH IS EXEMPLARY AND THE STYLING BREATHTAKING."

My first ever house purchase got in the way of me owning a Z1 – and I'm still regretting it now

Kawasaki's attention to detail was awesome. Not only was the Z1 an engineering masterpiece but every other part of the bike was of the same quality

production was set at a modest 1500 units a month. By 1975, 5000 Z1s were pouring from Kawasaki's production line every 30 days.

So what made the Kawasaki such a great motorcycle?

First and foremost it was, and is, utterly, lust inducingly gorgeous. The fit and finish is exemplary and the styling breathtaking. Instead of the big, fat, middle-aged car driver's fuel tank and saddle of the Honda, the Kwack looked light and slim. Incidentally, it wasn't, weighing in at a fully adult 540lb.

The kicked up, rear seat fairing, slim saddle and aggressive exhaust pipes looked like a motorcyclist's bike – a machine that you rushed home from work and just rode and rode and rode, simply because it was king of all it surveyed. On a Z1 you were top of the petrol powered tree – whether two or four wheels.

But the Kawasaki was far more than just a pretty face. The engineering was exemplary and very clever. Everything except really major maintenance could be done with the engine in the frame. The motor might have been dohc, normally the realm of GP racers of the day, but it was simple and totally indestructible in even hard use.

Kawasaki cut no corners in terms of the engine. The all roller bearing crankshaft was made up of nine individual components and was over-engineered even for racing. The eight-plate clutch was huge and unbreakable and the pinions in the five-speed

gearbox massive. Little wonder then, that these engines are still raced today.

The handling wasn't so good. In fact, it wasn't very good at all! The first major problem was the Dunlop Gold Seal tyres. They were absolute rubbish in the dry of California. In soggy England, they became lethal.

The rear dampers were a joke, the front forks very marginal and, even with a twin disc front end, riding the Kwack at near its 140mph potential top speed – and yes, they would run up to this sort of speed day in and day out – was a life-threatening exercise.

Another problem was a high-speed front end weave which then amplified to become a full blown tank-slapper, simply because the chassis – a fairly direct lift from the ill-handling two-stroke triples – was not up to the job of managing the big, heavy 80bhp engine. The steering damper on a Z1 was as essential as the bike's wheels or engine.

Riding a Z1 today is still a wonderful experience – right at the top of the classic bike tree. With modern tyres and decent rear dampers, the bike's handling is transformed and the big Kwack will waft effortlessly up to 80mph on a whiff of throttle, and cruise there all day long.

The Z1 is a practical bike too, being just as reliable as ever and with a fine supply of parts, many provided by Kawasaki's original suppliers.

The only downside is the price. The Z1's virtues are widely recognised and therefore you could expect to pay an eye-watering £15,000 for a really stunning Z1, Z1A or Z1B. ■

The remarkable
1919 Guzzi GP

MOTORCYCLING LIFE

THE MOTO GUZZI MUSEUM AT MANDELLO DEL LARIO

I had heard a lot about the Moto Guzzi Museum and was fascinated with the mystery behind it. For a start, it seems to be almost permanently closed and getting hard, factual information about the collection is very difficult – and that statement comes from a journalist whose job it is to find things out.

Eventually, I made contact with a press officer at Piaggio, which owns Moto Guzzi, who explained that there was no chance of the museum being open when I was in the area. None. "Sicuramente nessuna possibilità a tutti."

Then I played my only remaining card. Did they know that I had actually ridden the legendary eight-cylinder Moto Guzzi V8 Grand Prix racer – one of the very few people in the world ever to have had this privilege?

Suddenly, things became very different. "Yes, please do come Mr Melling. We'll open the museum just for you and give you your very own tour guide."

It was a wonderful experience.

»

Exhibits are laid
out very simply
in the Moto
Guzzi Museum

OBJECTIVITY: *The state or quality of being true even outside of a subject's individual biases, interpretations, feelings, and imaginings.*

Objectively I should say that the Moto Guzzi Museum, at Mandello del Lario on the banks of Lake Como in northern Italy, has relatively few motorcycles on display for a world class museum.

It is also important to add that the museum is housed in an old building, dating from the 1920s, and that the displays are plain and utilitarian.

And, in purely objective terms, visitor facilities are poor. Admission to the museum is free of charge and so there is no blank faced, and emotionally absent, ticket vendor to prepare the visitor for the shock which will soon assault them. There are no audio guides or booklets to lend a helping hand.

This is a museum fit only for the dedicated Moto Guzzi acolyte. Voyeurs, bystanders and tourists need to seek their historical thrills elsewhere.

All this is factually and objectively accurate. The tour is over. Now let's move on.

The problem is that I cannot move on, nor can I ever be objective about the Moto Guzzi Museum because, despite all its faults – or maybe even because of its foibles – this is a shrine not only to motorcycling but to human endeavour. Nowhere in the world will you see human creativity more clearly and overtly manifested than in this rather dowdy display of

motorcycles and motorcycle engineering.

You know that something special is about to happen when you enter Mandello del Lario. Like all the lakeside villages, towns and small cities in this sub-Alpine region, it is squeezed tight up against the mountains on one side and the water on the other. The difference is that Mandello del Lario proudly proclaims that it is: Citta dei Motori.

Drive a few hundred yards further along the narrow road and there on the left is a small, somewhat grubby car park but, uniquely in the world, it bears the plaque: Piazza Carlo Guzzi – for Mandello del Lario is Moto Guzzi and Moto Guzzi is Mandello del Lario, with each enjoying the mutually symbiotic relationship.

The Moto Guzzi factory was built in 1921 – and looks as if it was. The Piaggio Group, which now owns the Moto Guzzi brand, is starting to rebuild the site as Guzzi production ramps up, but the iron framed windows, carrying more than 90 years of paint, bear testimony that this is an authentically historic building.

The entry to the museum is anti-climactic in the extreme. There is no huge artwork proclaiming what the visitor is about to see; no theme park welcome from gleaming toothed hostesses and no offers to dine in an 'authentic' 1930s Italian restaurant. Instead one ascends a set of worn stairs and, quite suddenly, you are thrust into the presence of greatness. The

"THIS IS A MUSEUM FIT ONLY FOR THE DEDICATED MOTO GUZZI ACOLYTE. VOYEURS, BYSTANDERS AND TOURISTS NEED TO SEEK THEIR HISTORICAL THRILLS ELSEWHERE."

The amazing supercharged Tre engine

experience is almost the equivalent of finding Michelangelo's David standing in the corner of a garden ornament shop.

Tucked away in a glass case, on the left-hand side of the corridor, is Carlo Guzzi's first motorcycle and it represents the fanfare of trumpets which launches the show.

But first, a short digression. For something over 1.7 million years our ancient ancestors made axes formed from pieces of flint or obsidian. During this whole period, the design remained more or less the same. A piece of stone was fashioned into a shape which fitted inside the user's hand and was then used as a tool or weapon as the situation demanded.

Then, just a mere 100,000 years ago, someone came along and said: "You know, you could put that little hand axe into the end of a stick and make a spear, or an arrow or scraper or…" And technology was born.

But it took some enormous creative genius to say that what had been happening for a million-and-a-half years could have been improved – things could be different.

So when Carlo Guzzi produced his first motorcycle in 1919, it wasn't a modified bicycle with a proprietary engine bought in from Switzerland or England. Guzzi said that there was a better way of making a motorcycle than just adding an engine to a bicycle.

The better way was a forward facing, single-cylinder engine which could be air-cooled because it was in the correct place to catch the airflow. The engine had an overhead cam

and four valves so that it breathed well.

There was an outside flywheel, which came to be called 'The Bacon Slicer', so that the crankshaft was stiff and the motor had low vibration.

The primary drive was by gear, rather than chain, with a three-speed, unit construction gearbox and automatic lubrication at a time when riders were expected to pump oil to the engine manually. Guzzi did not so much improve motorcycle design as rip it to shreds and start from new. These same ideas were to dominate Guzzi's thinking for the next 50 years.

Carlo Guzzi was only able to develop his superior hand axes because his partner was Giorgio Parodi. Guzzi and Parodi had been colleagues in the Italian Servizio Aeronautica during the First World War and it was the Parodi family fortune, made from shipping and armaments, which bankrolled the whole project.

Guzzi was an aircraft mechanic and Parodi a pilot. A close friend and confidant of the pair was another flyer named Giovanni Ravelli. He was killed in 1919, just after the end of hostilities, but Guzzi and Parodi were determined to keep his memory alive by using the legendary soaring eagle on every motorcycle they made.

In fact, the first Guzzi is actually called a GP – to recognise the Guzzi/Parodi link – but the young Giorgio's family were so concerned about the adverse publicity if things went wrong with the new venture that they had the Parodi element of the name dropped and so Moto Guzzi was born. »

The legendary
V7 California as
used by the CHP

Guzzi was fortunate in having Parodi for a business partner because young Giorgio's dad, Emanuele Parodi, was a seriously smart businessman and made sure that if he was going to back the new motorcycle business it would be profitable.

Mr Parodi deemed the GP too complex and expensive to make and so, in 1921, the much simpler Moto Guzzi Normale went on sale and was the beginning of one of the outstanding success stories in Italian motorcycling.

Now, we tend to think of Moto Guzzi being a rather quirky, niche manufacturer but until the marque's decline in the 1970s, it was the most successful Italian motorcycle manufacturer with a stunning record of making popular, reliable motorcycles which customers wanted to buy.

After the GP, the next gallery proudly displays a Normale Norge which went to the Arctic Circle and the little Airone which was Italy's best-selling 250 for 16 years.

I was particularly impressed by Guzzi's own interpretation of a truly practical scooter which the factory first produced in 1950 – in direct response to a postwar Italy starved of personal transport.

The Galletto 160, carrying the nickname 'The Priest's Scooter', was a 160cc, 6hp machine which enabled the local priest – and there were

an awful lot of the clergy in Italy – to get around their parishes quickly, economically and safely, even on poorly made roads. With an alloy cylinder and barrel and, naturally, a horizontal engine, the Galletto was safe, easy to ride and a real workhorse – and it made Guzzi a huge amount of money.

The road bikes are remarkable but, for me, the visit was dominated by Guzzi's incredible range of racing motorcycles.

Guzzi's belief in mass centralisation and low drag gave them five consecutive 350cc world championships from 1953 to 1957.

These sweet handling single-cylinder machines, developed in Guzzi's own wind tunnel, allowed Fergus Anderson, Bill Lomas and Keith Campbell to carry enormous corner speed on the rough, public road circuits which formed the GP calendar in this period.

It is a joy to be able to get close to these wonderful bikes and admire the craftsmanship. I took a particular delight in looking at the magnesium alloy fairing on Lomas' bike which still shows the working of the English wheel and planishing hammer where the Guzzi craftsman stretched and beat the metal into shape more than six decades ago.

Not that Guzzi was addicted to single cylinder racing. Towards the end of the gallery,

The 1921 Moto Guzzi Normale – an instant sales success

there is a magnificent display of supercharged singles and V-twins – and the utterly sublime three cylinder 'Tre'.

In an act of incredible generosity and kindness, my hosts allowed me to cross the barrier and touch the Tre and to do so was a quasi-religious experience. The three inclined water-cooled cylinders would be state-of-the-art now – as would the neat supercharger tucked away above the engine. The 500cc engine produced 65hp at only 8000rpm so it is reasonable to think of 120hp-plus for a 1000cc engine – or about what a current sports touring machine is making. The difference is that the Guzzi dates from 1940.

Along with a science fiction sophisticated engine was a spine frame containing the engine's oil. Neat, compact, and barely any wider than a 500cc single, the Tre was destined for stardom except for the Fédération Internationale de Motocyclisme's ban on superchargers. I simply stood in awe next to it.

There is a huge display of Guzzis derived from the V7 military ATV engine and these are fascinating. Dr John Wittner's Daytona race bikes are magnificent, as is the regal Moto Guzzi California police bike. The problem with the V-twin displays is that they are too near to the one reason why you should, must, make

the journey to Mandello del Lario because you are about to come into the presence of greatness.

There on an imperially raised dais – as well it might be – is the Moto Guzzi Otto Cilindri: Giulio Cesare Carcano's legendary V8.

Carcano joined Moto Guzzi in 1936 and worked alongside Mr Guzzi until they decided that the single-cylinder race bikes could never compete against the fours of Gilera and MV Agusta. In another smashing of the hand axe, Carcano designed an eight-cylinder racing motorcycle which was so neat, small, and aerodynamic that it looked barely bigger than the singles it replaced.

With a top speed in excess of 175mph in 1957 – so fast that Guzzi's factory riders did everything they could to avoid racing the machine – the 'Otto' would have been a motorcycle racing legend had Guzzi not withdrawn from GP racing in 1957.

Incredibly, you can stand inches away from the V8 and get even closer to the eight-cylinder engines displayed in the gallery.

There are many fine motorcycling museums but, regardless of the effort, this is one you must visit.

My thanks to Fabio and Walther for all their help with this story. ■

MOTO GUZZI

The Guzzi wasn't difficult to ride, but racing it at 175mph would have been a very different matter

V8

ONCE IN EVERY LIFETIME, COMES A CHANCE LIKE THIS ... (WITH APOLOGIES TO CLIFF RICHARD)

Gather motojournalists together and they can be just a bit bitchy. 'I've ridden this', and 'I've ridden that', and 'what have you got on your testing cv?' Although I am some galaxies away from an angel in white leathers, adorned with a shining, titanium race halo, I do tend to stay quiet in these conversations for the very simple reason that I can always, but always, win... because I've actually ridden the legendary eight cylinder Moto Guzzi V8.

The Guzzi V8 was so incredibly advanced that it would be state-of-the-art today. Yet the motorcycle was conceived 62 years ago by Giulio Cesare Carcano – who is arguably the greatest motorcycle designer of all time.

I rode it thanks to the generosity of Sammy Miller, who has been kind enough to trust me with many of the priceless exhibits in his museum.

But the Moto Guzzi is at the top of the tree and I still get goose bumps thinking about the bike: it was incredible.

ENTRANCE

Moto Guzzi V8 – underneath that huge dustbin fairing, the V8 is tiny for a 500

The Moto Guzzi V8 is wheeled out of Sammy Miller's workshop and into the courtyard of his museum. Immediately, a group of grey haired enthusiasts gather round the bike. Eight cylinders – each with its own carburettor. Sixteen valves, two banks of camshafts. Oil in the frame for cooling and mass centralisation, and with a top speed timed at 178mph... a bike which would take on a current Superbike, despite being only 500cc.

This is no ordinary motorcycle.

One of the aficionados stands proudly by the Guzzi – but still a respectful distance from this motorcycling legend. He pulls in his ample belly and stands up straight like a Grenadier Guard coming to attention. He knows he is in the presence of magic. He tells his mates: "I've waited all my life to have my picture taken next to that bike. I can die happy now."

I don't tell him that in less than an hour I won't be standing next to the Guzzi, but riding it. Like him, I am in awe of this motorcycle.

As I pull on my leathers I am nervous, very nervous. I never doubt my ability to ride exotic bikes but the Guzzi isn't just exotic – it is a legend in metal. Maybe 10 or so people in the world have ever ridden a Guzzi V8. As for the cost of repairing the bike if I make a mistake – think of any figure and then start adding zeros... lots and lots of them!

You just can't press the starter button on the V8 and ride off. It has to be treated with respect. First John Ring, Sammy's race mechanic, gives each carburettor an individual squirt of heavily leaded race fuel, then Bob Stanley, who rebuilds all the bikes in the Miller museum, backs the

V8 on to the starter, spins the rollers and brings the V8 coughing into life rather like a Rolls-Royce Merlin engine firing up on a Spitfire.

After 10 seconds, all eight cylinders are running and the eight, completely unsilenced exhausts are singing together. Like everything else on this bike, the sound is unique. It's not nearly so harsh as the Gilera and MV fours I know so well and is much less strident than the multi cylinder engines from Honda. In fact, it is almost civilised.

Lacking anything worth calling a flywheel, the V8 will stall in an instant so Bob blips the throttle constantly, keeping the revs between 5000 and 6000. It's a skilled job because the V8 is water-cooled, unlike all the other great bikes of its era, so it has to be warmed up carefully. Run the bike too cold and it will seize. Run it too hot and it will also seize. This is not a beginner's classic race bike.

From the outside, the Guzzi looks awkward and almost home-made. But Carcano was an engineers' engineer and never a stylist. For him, function was all and so the V8 will never win any beauty competition.

However, once on the bike, the hand beaten aluminium fuel tank with all its strange curves

Carcano's V8 was pure functional engineering with no thought to aesthetics

and cutaways moulds around my knees like a tailor-made suit. It's the same with the padded leather seat which doesn't so much push the rider into the tank as holds them there. There is only one riding position on offer, but it is a comfortable one and ideal for racing.

After the tension of the build-up, taking off on the Guzzi is a real anti-climax. The motor is so torquey and easy to use that you could go shopping on the V8. The clutch is light and perfectly judged for bite and once over 10mph the bike has perfect, effortless balance.

In a few yards, I start to give the V8 its head and I'm rewarded with a rev counter needle which swings round at lightning speed and a baritone wail which arrows into my soul.

Conscious of the bill if the motor drops a valve, or seizes, I change gear at 12,000rpm, rather than the 13,000+ the works riders used,

and the acceleration is superb. The V8 is not dramatically better than the MVs and Gileras – it's not even worth mentioning the single cylinder Manx Nortons against which it competed – but it is a much easier ride. Open the throttle, 12,000rpm and slide in the next gear. It's all smooth and easy and the motor is just so willing.

With modern tyres the handling is rock solid over the bumps and undulations of the old airstrip which we are using for a test track, and the huge, double sided, twin leading shoe brakes scrub off speed effortlessly. What wouldn't I give to actually race this bike?

Riding at 150mph, with a full fairing and the rock hard tyres of 1957 would have been a different matter and it's not surprising that Guzzi's factory riders were often reluctant heroes when it came to racing the V8. »

"AS I PULL ON MY LEATHERS I AM NERVOUS, VERY NERVOUS. I NEVER DOUBT MY ABILITY TO RIDE EXOTIC BIKES BUT THE GUZZI ISN'T JUST EXOTIC – IT IS A LEGEND"

"THE MOST AMAZING THING ABOUT THE GUZZI V8 IS THAT IT WENT FROM A BLANK SHEET OF PAPER TO A RUNNING ENGINE IN JUST FIVE MONTHS."

So, if the Guzzi was so good why didn't it win everything? The primary problem with the bike was the ignition. On the original bike, Carcano had eight individual sets of mechanically opened points for the eight cylinders, and getting them to work in harmony was very difficult. Now, Sammy's V8 has electronic ignition and this explains why the bike runs so well.

The bike also suffered from chronic overheating caused by the extremely compact layout of the engine and the 'dustbin' fairing which, while being ultra-slippery in terms of aerodynamics, provided poor air flow for the radiator.

Guzzi was also hugely underfunded and, despite Carcano's genius, the race team was a real budget exercise. Finally Guzzi withdrew from racing in 1957, just as the V8 was getting sorted. Given another year, and a decent

funding, there would have been nothing in the world to touch the bike.

But there was no increase in budget, and no next year either, so the V8 remains one of the great 'what ifs' of racing.

So what was the story of the man behind it, Giulio Cesare Carcano?

Perhaps the most amazing thing about the Guzzi V8 is that Carcano took it from a blank sheet of paper to a running engine in just five months. It's also important to remember that there were no computer predictions or simulations available to Moto Guzzi. He sat down at his desk with a pencil, a sheet of paper and a simple slide rule calculator as the only aids to his creative genius. Everything else happened inside his head.

A team of Guzzi engineers worked on the project but they were led by the creative genius of Giulio Cesare Carcano who began work

Regardless of all the other incredible bikes I have ridden, the V8 is at the top of the tree

Carcano's tiny V8 is the work of a genius

The steering head runs through the centre of the huge, oil bearing spine frame and gives an extremely stiff design

> A total of eight sets of mechanically operated points live behind the two alloy covers at the top of the engine. It was too much to ask of 1950s technology

at Moto Guzzi, writing workshop manuals, in 1936. But, like many ambitious young engineers before him, Carcano had racing in his heart and in 1938 began working with Carlo Guzzi on the company's light, narrow and agile 500cc singles. This bike, and the ideas behind it, stayed with Carcano all the way to the V8.

He was right to be influenced by the horizontal engined Guzzis because they won five consecutive 350cc world championships, from 1953 to 1957. In one of his last interviews, Carcano said: "The 350 was an agile and reliable motorcycle and was competitive against the four cylinder bikes (from MV Agusta and Gilera) which gave 10 more horsepower but were 40lb (18kg) heavier."

So, when Carcano began work on the V8 it was lightness and a narrow frontal area which dominated his thinking. Why then did he go down the route of eight cylinders rather than the proven four cylinder engines of MV and Gilera?

"We thought differently. Once we abandoned our singles and V twins, the obvious solution would be four cylinders.

"But building a four cylinder meant staying behind Gilera and MV, because they started earlier and we would have had to work at least a couple of years to be at the same level of experience and development.

"Then we thought that if we were aiming for eight cylinders the power was not an issue anymore. On the contrary, weight and dimensions would be important. Our eight »

The V8 is a lot more comfortable, and spacious, than it looks from the outside

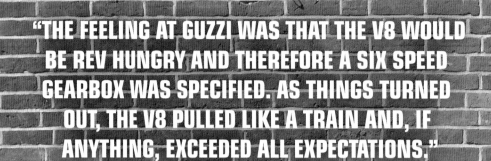

"THE FEELING AT GUZZI WAS THAT THE V8 WOULD BE REV HUNGRY AND THEREFORE A SIX SPEED GEARBOX WAS SPECIFIED. AS THINGS TURNED OUT, THE V8 PULLED LIKE A TRAIN AND, IF ANYTHING, EXCEEDED ALL EXPECTATIONS."

The V8 is surprisingly slim. With a little more time, and investment, it could have been the most successful GP racer ever

The beautiful, hand beaten magnesium alloy fuel tank is a work of art

Unusually for the Golden Age of GP racing, the V8 is watercooled and the temperature gauge is vital

cylinder was brilliant because it was no bigger than a 250cc bike.

"When it was tested on the bench for the first time it already gave 63hp while the Gilera gave 60hp... and we were just at the very first tests.

"Then it achieved 70-72hp and the power would be increased more and more if they did not kill it with the famous 1957 agreement."

Carcano was as good as his word and built a tiny V8 with a crankshaft just 13½in wide (342mm) and the whole bike weighing only 330lb (150kg), which is a less than the weight of a current MotoGP bike.

Confident as he was of his ability and his predictions – and Carcano really was – the feeling at Guzzi was that the V8 would be rev hungry and therefore a six speed gearbox was specified. As things turned out, the V8 pulled like a train and, if anything, exceeded all expectations.

The bike's problems were two-fold. First, Carcano's ideas were right on the very, very edge of what was possible with the technology of the day and, in particular, there was no way of reliably delivering the 800 sparks a second which the V8 required.

In tandem with Carcano's ambition outstretching the limits of 1953 technology, the race department at Moto Guzzi was woefully underfunded and development took place irregularly.

Carcano said: "If you think about modern factories, Guzzi's organisation of that time will make you shudder!

"For example, the racing department didn't even have a workshop of its own. We had our own staff managing the racing but for the rest it depended on the production department.

"The toolmaker department, which normally produced the tools for production

motorcycles, had to work also for us and we, in the racing department, had always to beg them for favours to do parts for us. It was a continuous battle.

"Moto Guzzi was not an organisation dedicated to the races as for example today in Ferrari. We depended on the toolmakers and production staff to help us with personal favours to get things made. It was impossible to race properly and professionally like this."

Emotionally, I want to believe that Carcano's genius would have been rewarded if Guzzi had stayed in GP racing for just one more year. However, intellectually, I have doubts.

The way Moto Guzzi went racing was completely normal for the time. The BSA competition department was known as a 'den of professional thieves' because of their proclivity for stealing parts from the production line and bribing skilled machinists to make race parts with free tickets for major events.

Norton and Gilera were no better, while Ducati was in an even worse state.

The only exception was MV Agusta, where racing motorcycles was Count Domenico Agusta's hobby and was funded by his highly profitable Bell Agusta helicopter business, so even MV was not a truly professional exercise.

It took Honda, which entered four riders in the 1959 TT, to show the world what real factory racing meant with dedicated designers and race bike production staff – and a virtually blank cheque to support them.

Probably, Carcano would have continued to struggle with Guzzi in 1958 – predominantly because of the ignition problems the high revving eight cylinder bike posed. What he needed was Soichiro Honda at his side... but that really would be re-writing history. ■

SUZUKI RE5

WHEN ENGINEERS START BELIEVING THEIR OWN PRESS RELEASES

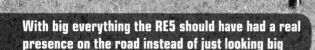

With big everything the RE5 should have had a real presence on the road instead of just looking big

Suzuki engineering staff embraced the Wankel concept enthusiastically

I don't actually dislike the RE5, as I do the Honda DN-01, but rather I feel a sense of sadness for Suzuki because it shows what happens when you let engineers have free, unfettered control of a project. With complete certainty, they will screw the job up – just in the same way that marketeers or stylists shouldn't be given a free rein either. For sure, great motorcycles are a team effort.

The RE5 was an epic piece of engineering – but a Titanic-sized catastrophe for Suzuki too and makes one of the most interesting stories in the history of motorcycling.

Motorcycles fail for many reasons. Research and development can be lacking, production facilities inadequate or the launch of the bike poorly executed. Rarely, very rarely indeed, a manufacturer can do everything right and still have a sales disaster on its hands. The Suzuki RE5 Wankel is such a motorcycle – a catastrophe of epic proportions – so much so that it actually threatened the very existence of the Suzuki factory.

The biggest problem with the RE5 is that the engineers actually did believe their own press releases and, worse than this, they convinced Suzuki management that all their equations, graphs and computer analyses were going to lead to a sales bonanza, the like of which Suzuki had never seen in its, then 50 year history. They were wrong.

The problems began at first base – and then grew exponentially. The Suzuki RE5 has a swept volume of 497cc – an archetypal capacity for a BSA Gold Star, Manx Norton or any other traditional British super sports single. Except that Suzuki sold the RE5 as a 1000cc sports tourer twin, when its actual capacity was 1491cc. Or maybe not…

Merely working out just what they were buying was the first of many, many problems facing the very few customers who jumped into the Wankel-engined maelstrom in 1974.

However, before discussing the motorcycle it needs putting into a social and historical context, because without this background the RE5 makes no sense whatsoever.

Honda, Yamaha and Suzuki all withdrew from grand prix racing at the end of the 1968 season. In that decade, the Japanese had proven themselves masters of technological innovation with everything from Honda's iconic, six-cylinder 250cc and 297cc jewels to the wondrous, but unraced, three-cylinder 50 produced by Suzuki. Yamaha was also well in the frame with its four-cylinder 125 and 250 world championship-winning two-strokes.

Suzuki president Jitsujiro Suzuki really bought the Wankel sales pitch from the engineers

So, except for MV, and MZ to a far lesser extent, if the rider of the day thought about state-of-the-art technology his default position was Japanese.

With the end of Japanese GP participation, brought about entirely by the stupidity and narcissism of the FIM, the Japanese lacked a showcase for their skills.

At precisely the same time, the world was an exciting place for engineers. In 1969, both Concorde and Boeing's 747 made their first flights. Neil Armstrong set foot on the moon on July 20 the same year – changing history forever.

As an aside, I missed Woodstock, Jimi Hendrix and The Who because, at the time, I was penniless and so had to be a surrogate hippy and comb my shoulder-length hair in a council house bedroom in a northern industrial town – which was not much of a substitute for joining my 500,000 fellow flower people in upstate New York.

Now, back to the story. In this febrile, can-do-anything atmosphere engineers in all the Japanese factories became very excited and the thing which enthused them most of all was the Holy Grail of the internal combustion engine – a power plant with, theoretically at least, virtually no moving parts or friction. Enter centre stage the Wankel engine.

Engineers really do love Wankel engines because the concept appeals to their inner purity. Talk to any engineer about what excites him, and increasingly her, and they will radiate joy at things which work wonderfully well and have supreme simplicity. On paper, the Wankel engine is just such a creation.

The idea is that a rotor, shaped rather like a three-sided wedge of cheese, spins round inside an oval-shaped chamber. A shaft is mounted eccentrically through the cheese wedge, rather like the camshaft on a four-stroke engine. The volume of each chamber changes as the rotor spins round so the fuel/air charge can be sucked in through a port in the wall of the oval

At the launch the RE5 engine looked real 21st century hi-tech

chamber, in the manner of a two-stroke. In the second part of the chamber, the charge is ignited and finally it exhausts through a port, again two-stroke style.

As the engine burns the air/fuel mix it turns the shaft and power is produced – truly elegant engineering.

Wankel advocates play some interesting political games with a rotary engine's size. When it suits them, they will claim that the capacity of a Wankel is represented by the internal volume of one of the rotor's segments. In the case of the RE5, this is 497cc. However, no one was ever going to pay big bike money for a 497cc engine so Suzuki claimed that the RE5 was actually a 1000cc multi. I could never quite follow this logic, even if it was demanded by some regulatory authorities. If the capacity of the whole engine was to be measured then surely it should have been a 1491cc triple rather than a 994cc twin.

I think the reason that it wasn't so branded was purely a marketing one. A 1500cc bike producing only 67hp and a feeble 54.9lb-ft of torque was a guaranteed sales failure before it ever reached the showroom.

Why then not sell it as a hot performing 497cc single? The problem here was the price point. In the key American market Suzuki wanted $2475 (£1980) for the RE5 which was almost a third more expensive than the stunning Kawasaki Z1 with a price ticket of $1895 (£1516) – a bike which would slaughter the RE5 in every single department.

"... A POWER PLANT WITH, THEORETICALLY AT LEAST, VIRTUALLY NO MOVING PARTS OR FRICTION. ENTER CENTRE STAGE THE WANKEL ENGINE."

How the Rotary Engine Functions

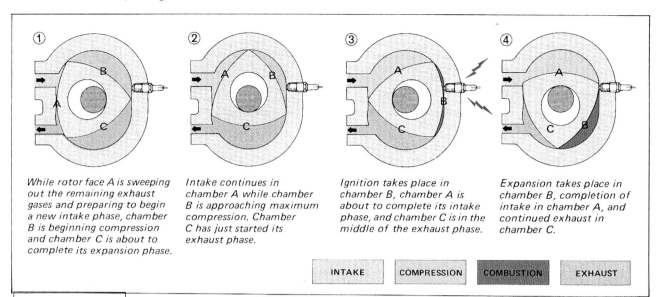

① While rotor face A is sweeping out the remaining exhaust gases and preparing to begin a new intake phase, chamber B is beginning compression and chamber C is about to complete its expansion phase.

② Intake continues in chamber A while chamber B is approaching maximum compression. Chamber C has just started its exhaust phase.

③ Ignition takes place in chamber B, chamber A is about to complete its intake phase, and chamber C is in the middle of the exhaust phase.

④ Expansion takes place in chamber B, completion of intake in chamber A, and continued exhaust in chamber C.

INTAKE | COMPRESSION | COMBUSTION | EXHAUST

"IN FACT, WITH ONLY ONE MOVING PART, THE WANKEL ENGINE IS A WONDER OF SIMPLICITY AND ENGINEERING ELEGANCE. EXCEPT THAT IT ISN'T. THE PROBLEMS ARE MANIFOLD AND SERIOUS TOO."

The Wankel cycle – theoretically simple but horrendously complex in practice

Honda's wonderful 750K3, a somewhat closer competitor in terms of performance (if only when viewed through the eyes of a Wankel fan), was only $1495 (£1196) – heading towards half the price of the RE5.

So, before anyone had even ridden an RE5, Suzuki was boxed into a real cost versus perceived value corner.

Like a lot of internal combustion engines, the Wankel origins are German. In 1919, the 17-year-old Felix Wankel was pondering how to make a simpler and more efficient engine than the burgeoning two- and four-strokes which were appearing everywhere. The problem was that the young Felix's dreams were far ahead of the available technology.

Regardless, he obtained his initial patent in 1929 but it was 28 years later, in 1957, that a practical rotary engine was first produced by the German NSU company.

On paper, the engine is a delight. There are no four-stroke valves boinging up and down and a complete absence of two-stroke disc-valves whirring round and round. In fact, with only one moving part, the Wankel engine is a wonder of simplicity and engineering elegance. Except that it isn't. The problems are manifold and serious too.

First, the tips of the rotors have to seal perfectly on the combustion chamber – and at high speeds. To achieve this seal, there is a spring loaded tip on the end of each arm of the rotor. These tips have to make perfect contact with the combustion chamber and so have to be extremely hard and durable. Clearly, the combustion chamber has to be hard too, and this is difficult to achieve.

In Suzuki's case, the solution was to purchase the coating technology from the US firm Platecraft, and this wasn't cheap.

Despite the apparent simplicity of the rotary engine, it's not efficient – particularly at lower rpm. To get the RE5 to make reasonable torque, Suzuki designed a combustion chamber with multiple ports to mimic the boost ports which it knew all too well from the two-stroke technology it had taken from MZ in 1961.

However, boost ports weren't sufficient on their own and Mikuni was commissioned to produce a unique, two-stage carburettor which constricted the available fuel and air at low rpm and then made more available as the revs increased. Simple engines? No, not really.

Then there was the major issue of the heat generated during the Wankel cycle. Rotary engines run hot – incredibly so – which is why the RE5 was made to be water and oil-cooled from the outset.

A further issue with water-cooling a motorcycle engine and then putting it into an unfaired bike is that, aesthetically, it looks like a generator or car power plant.

Not that the challenges finished there.

The exhaust gases produced by the RE5 were so hot that a double skinned exhaust had to be used – and even then this had to be force fed

Suzuki RE5 front forks and brakes were lifted from the GT750 and were anything but hi-tech

with air, via two ducts at the front of the bike.

As the engine got nearer to production Suzuki increasingly found that Wankel simplicity did not equate to conventional engineering simplicity. Three separate oiling systems were needed to make the engine reliable. One was total loss, for the rotor tips, and this was an immediate cause for concern because the first glimmers of the rising environmental impact sun were starting to be seen on the horizon. A second, completely separate lubrication system looked after the main bearings while a third lubed the gearbox.

In order to operate the dual stage carburettor and the lubrication system, a total of five separate cables had to be opened and closed by the throttle. How simple do you want simple to be?

The final result of the engineering was a hugely complex motorcycle which was

Suzuki RE5 had an engine which was not motorcycle art. Presumably its engineer parents were proud

Sexy key fob – shame about the bike

expensive to produce and didn't stack up in terms of performance.

Could things get any worse? Actually, yes they could.

At this point in the story it's important to stress the social and historical context of Suzuki's Wankel. When project chief Shigeyasu Kamiya launched the RE5 programme both Honda and Yamaha were also actively developing Wankels of their own. In fact, Yamaha got as far as producing the first batch of tooling for a twin rotor design.

At the launch, Jitsujiro Suzuki, president of the Suzuki Motor Company, had the light truly shining in his eyes when he said: "Our success in realising the RE5 would not have been possible without the strong pioneer spirit that has characterised Suzuki since its establishment. But just as much, it relies on our motto: 'To Make Products of Value.'

"More than an adventure in advanced technology, the Suzuki RE5 faithfully reflects our wish to respond to the needs of the user, in terms of operational performance and comfort."

The Suzuki PR staff were just as evangelical: "The RE5 is confirmation that the several advantages of the rotary type internal combustion engine – smoothness in operation, low vibration, a small number of moving parts greatly reducing maintenance problems…"

And so the eulogy went on and on, in the way which only true missionaries can.

Oh dear! »

In Britain, the BSA group had already committed to a twin rotor Wankel as its saviour for the future. In every way, the signposts were pointing towards a rotary future.

For its part, Suzuki put the necessary tens of millions of pounds, in terms of engineering and capital investment, to make the RE5 a success. For example, a brand-new, unique production line was built at Hammatsu.

Mr Kamiya then bought in the world-leading, Italian stylist Giorgetto Giugiaro to give the highest of hi-tech looks to the bike. For example, Giugiaro had the instrument panels covered by a translucent green cover which rolled back, Star Trek style, to reveal – well, a pair of very ordinary analogue clocks.

Then customers got their hands on the bike…

The actual RE5 launch was fronted by American astronaut Ed Mitchell, who extolled the virtues of this cutting edge motorcycle. However, engine apart, the bike actually wasn't that advanced. The gearbox was lifted from the Suzuki GT750 triple and was only a five-speeder, and the extremely conventional chassis struggled to deal with the problem of the huge, heavy lump of an engine which had to be mounted very high in the frame.

Suzuki then gave the bike a long, 59in wheelbase to add stability, which it did, but this accentuated the bike's already porky size even more.

Suzuki dealers worldwide were told to go flat out with their own consumer launches. Martin Crooks, then a 14 year old working after school in his dad's Crooks Suzuki dealership – at the time the biggest Suzuki franchise in Britain – remembers the launch well.

"Eddie (Martin's dad) hired the Civic Hall in Barrow and we showed off the RE5 which Suzuki told us we had to stock. There was loads of interest but no one wanted to part with their own money.

"Eddie was keen on the RE5 because he'd already owned a Wankel-engined NSU car but even with his enthusiasm, he couldn't convince customers to buy it.

"Eventually, we got rid of the one bike and we were glad to see it go.

"We still had a whole board full of Suzuki special tools, which I wish I had been able to keep, but they all got destroyed in a fire so we really never did make any profit from the RE5 project."

So, despite all the glitz and glamour of a very posh launch, the RE5 was a sales disaster. Crooks Suzuki was not the only one to hit a concrete wall in terms of sales. Only 65 RE5s were sold in the crucial German market during 1975 and, as the bike's reputation developed, this fell to one – as in a single unit – in 1976.

If the RE5 was a complex beast in the hands of Suzuki development staff, it proved to be plutonium toxic for normal customers. A key problem was the unique NGK A9EFP spark plug. This had a fondness for oiling up, at which point the bike wouldn't start, and replacement plugs were difficult to obtain as well as expensive.

Then there was the issue of getting all five cables correctly adjusted and keeping a close eye on the three separate oil reservoirs.

But none of these issues was the deal breaker in the bike's success or, as things transpired, its failure. I have met a few Wankel engineers over the years and they all make one crucial mistake. It is to assume that while rotary engine technology will develop, four-stroke designs will remain static.

While Suzuki was ram-raiding its cash reserves for the RE5 project it was also developing the truly delightful four-cylinder, four-stroke GS750. This bike produced 72hp compared with the 67hp of the RE5, made more torque, weighed slightly less and sold at $2195 (£1756) in the US – almost 10% cheaper than the Wankel.

The GS750 also handled vastly better than the RE5 and could be ridden ruthlessly, flat out – all day every day without missing a beat. Suzuki dealers were soon queuing up for the new in-line four, and desperately trying to

Unfortunately, the RE5 does not have a good side. From every angle, the bike is wrong

bury any RE5s they had in stock by doing ridiculous deals. A chap I knew through racing actually swapped a suit of replica medieval armour, and not a very good one either, for an RE5 – and then immediately regretted the deal.

It was this armour-generated bike that I rode for a couple of hours in 1977 and my overwhelming memory was of wasting a nice afternoon, when I could have been doing something which was much more fun.

The only thing of interest was the very attractive, burbling Wankel note – always unmistakable if you have ridden a rotary engined motorcycle. The rest of the experience was memorable for its dullness. There wasn't much power, and the bike's owner had given me severe warnings about the dangers of over-revving the motor, while the handling continued the theme of utter ordinariness.

Would anyone pay a premium to own a bike like this, even if it were the best looking and most reliable motorcycle ever made? The

answer was unequivocally in the negative.

Today, the RE5 continues to attract near fanatical loyalty from its acolytes – in the way that quirky motorcycles tend to do. However, the market place tells the true story. There are any number of RE5s on offer, for less money than you would pay for a nice 250 BSA or Triumph – and that says it all. ■

Air vents forced cooling air down the double skinned exhaust pipes in an attempt to keep them cool

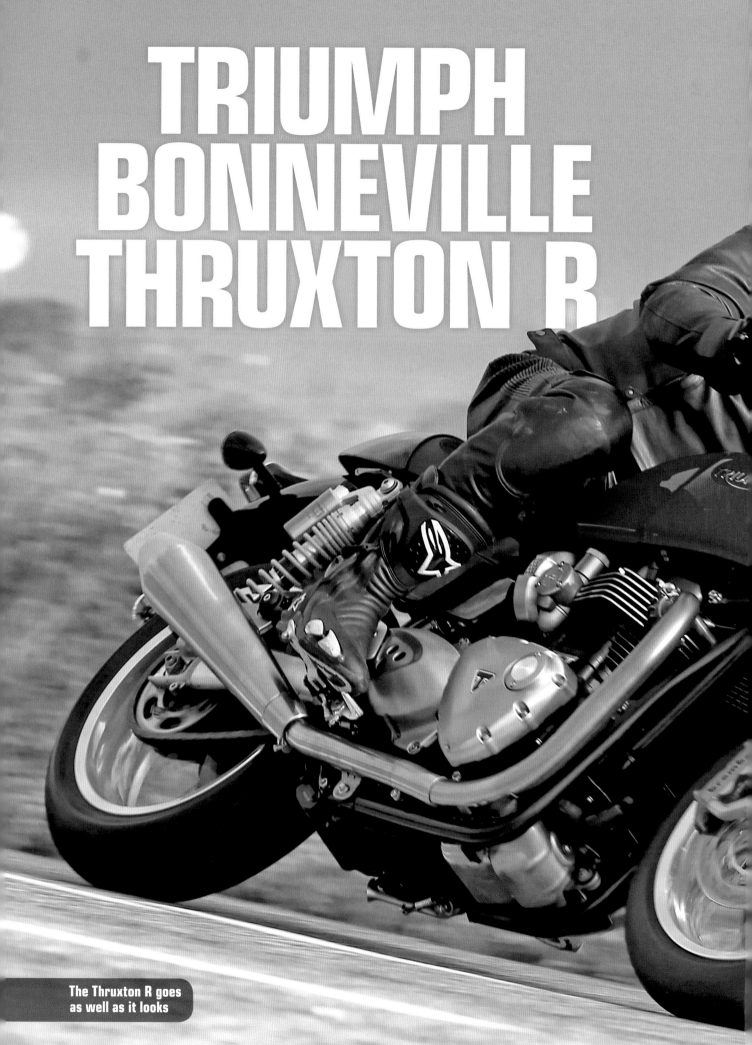

TRIUMPH BONNEVILLE THRUXTON R

The Thruxton R goes
as well as it looks

A TRUE MODERN CLASSIC

At the time I wrote this story, I was very much on Triumph's Christmas card list, so I was invited to the launch of the Bonneville range in Portugal. Despite being a really rushed affair even by hectic current standards, and brass monkey cold, the Thruxton R was amazing. It's by far the nicest bike in the Bonneville range and Triumph has pulled off the cleverest of all tricks in making a thoroughly modern bike which still has its classic DNA shining through every pore.

The only thing which is bizarre is that Triumph refused to do a GT version of the bike with an upright riding position and a dual seat. Off the record, Triumph staff said that their Italian importer in particular had been screaming for just such a bike, but it hasn't happened so far. That's why we own our Ducati GT1000 and not a Thruxton R! »

The R uses the same engine as the rest of the Bonneville line but with lighter crank, higher compression and model specific engine mapping

f you're in a rush, and want to go out riding rather than read stories in books, I'll come straight to the point. The Triumph Thruxton R is not only the best ever Retro bike made, it's a great motorcycle by any standards.

If you love classics, you'll sell your kidney for this bike. If you are thirtysomething, then you'll be trading in your R1, or Fireblade, to own an R. In short, the bike is this good and Triumph dealers all over the world will confirm the fact, as the Rs have been flying out of their showrooms in manic numbers.

The Thruxton R is at the top of the Bonneville family tree but still shares the majority of the family gene pool with the 900cc Street Twin and its even more closely related sibling, the 1200cc T120 Bonneville. So, at the heart of the R is the same twin cylinder, eight-valve engine with twin counter balancers and 270° firing order. The result is a thoroughly modern, vibration-free engine which could almost have a personality as the big, 97.6mm pistons bang up and down in the barrels. It's a really clever job that Triumph has done, melding an authentically classic feel into something which younger riders will also find acceptable.

The engine is liquid cooled, a concept which is both for marketing and practical reasons. In terms of selling the R there is no doubt that having the big, angular fins stuck out into the breeze like a real Meriden Bonnie is a priceless attraction. Equally, the finning does

cool the engine so the radiator can be tiny and unobtrusive. Tucked away between the front down tubes on the frame, it's not much larger than an oil cooler.

The catalyser, now compulsory to get through Euro 4 regulations, is hidden beneath the engine and the plumbing is equally well concealed. If you wish, it's easy to find the engineering and have a really good sigh and grumble about modern regulations but, equally, if you just want to ride the R, or pretend that this is really one of Doug Hele's Meriden creations, then you can do this too.

Just as neat is a sweet, six-speed gearbox with an extremely light clutch action thanks to Triumph's assist slipper clutch. Yet again, the Hinckley team has managed to be all

things to all buyers with this bike. Other than having the gear shift on the left-hand side – a true heresy for a hard core British classic bike acolyte – the box is even better than the hand-built, factory prepared production racing Bonneville I rode.

The R's exhaust note was the subject of some controversy at the launch. Because of the change in the way exhaust sound is measured under Euro 4 regulations, it is actually much nicer and quite reminiscent of a Meriden Bonnie in a way which the emasculated T100 Bonneville, the predecessor of the R, never was. The R makes a lovely growl which is involving, pleasant and which, unless you drop the clutch at 8000 rpm and wheel spin up the road outside your house, won't upset anyone. »

Retro or not, the Thruxton would be a lot of fun on a track day

"CRITICALLY, FOR CHILDREN OF ALL AGES, THE R WILL POWER WHEELIE IN THE FIRST TWO GEARS, AND WHAT MORE COULD ONE ASK?"

However, the feeling among younger journalists was that this wasn't sufficiently 'real' – whatever that word means – and the standard silencer was considered to be a bit of a woosie. Triumph agreed and offers Vance and Hines exhausts as accessories. These are simply offensively loud and will get right up the nose of every non-motorcyclist. Those whom the Gods would destroy, they first make mad…

Triumph is selling the Bonneville as a life-style machine, so will no doubt be proud that mentally challenged members of this new community can annoy the general public with factory fitted noise generators just as much as muppets on Harleys manage to with their exhausts. And then the industry wonders why motorcycles are selected for intrusive and restrictive legislation.

The accessories are a big deal for Triumph, and I do mean a seriously major target. It's not only the range of accessories which is impressive but the way they are being marketed. There are in excess of 160 individual items offered, ranging from what Triumph calls 'inspiration kits' to bullet indicators. This is very Harley territory, but what is clever is the way the accessories are being sold.

The Thruxton is beautifully proportioned

The idea is that you hand over your £12,000 – and no, don't even think of asking for a discount because the answer will be negative – and then sit down with the salesman and make your R personal. Your Triumph dealer will quote a fixed price for the accessories and the fitting. It will be very, very easy to add another couple of thousand pounds to the base price.

If you want to be an independent customiser, then this is easy too. Triumph has made nearly all the bling easily fitted, on any Saturday morning, using your home tool kit. No cutting, grinding or need for a TIG welder.

Finally, all the parts are Triumph guaranteed, road legal and do not adversely affect the bike's warranty. Truly a case of (and apologies to Brian Wilson and Mike Love) "You're gonna have fun, fun, fun until your wife takes the credit card away…"

Although it's billed as the rooty-tooty super sports bike in the Bonneville range, in the real world the R is the easiest and most pleasant of the three new bikes – even with a lighter crankshaft and higher compression than the standard T120 Black.

With 95hp on the end of the ride-by-wire throttle, there is ample power to lose your

The Thruxton is not only a great Retro bike but one of the best all round motorcycles of its generation

licence, and without making any effort. Counterintuitively it is actually smoother and easier to ride than the T120 Bonneville, with completely linear power delivery. Given a choice of the two engines for either touring or commuting I would take the R every time.

All new Bonneville engines are light on fuel and the R is no exception. Even hammering the bike in Portugal, in a way which would stretch the goodwill and tolerance of your local constabulary if you rode like this in Britain, 50+mpg is easily achievable. Two-up and ambling around looking at the scenery you can expect even better than this figure.

The power is creamy smooth and helped by some subtle electronics. There is both ABS and traction control. I can't see a reason for not using either of these aids. It's a bit like saying that in the good old days, Dunlop TT100 tyres were the only rubber to use. This was true but compared with a modern tyre, a TT100 is fit only for wheelbarrows. Why not make use of current technology if it doesn't interfere with the riding experience?

Critically, for children of all ages, the R will power wheelie in the first two gears, and what more could one ask?

There is a particularly relevant reason for having ABS. The R comes with a pair of magnificent 320mm front discs carrying Brembo four-piston, radially-mounted, Monobloc callipers. Oooooooooooohhhh, these are truly fantasy inducingly magnificent. Simply rest your middle finger on the lightweight, alloy front brake lever and it's like hitting a science fiction force field of speed reduction.

Just as good is that the stoppers are ultra-sensitive. Trail brake all the way, right up to the apex of the bend and then whack on the power—and move out of the way young Mr Rossi! I really did have a lot of fun playing GP racing.

The chassis data indicates that the R should be a flighty, nervous beast. It has a short 55.7in (1415mm) wheelbase and the steering head angle is sports bike steep at 22.8°. Yet, on the road, the results are completely different. The R can be eased into corners almost degree by degree and will respond with laser accuracy. Alternatively, it can be chucked around in true, sports bike style. I'd run this bike in the intermediate group of any track day and feel very happy that I wouldn't get in anyone's way—and that's for sure.

Clearly, the steering geometry is the key   »

factor in the sublime handling but the numbers are made to work with an 'upside down' floating piston, Showa front suspension and a pair of very competent Öhlin shocks on the rear.

In practice, these provide instant feedback on what is happening to the 17in Diablo Rosso Corsa tyres and, although firm, they will still soak up big pot holes – and there were more than a few of these on the poorly surfaced Portuguese roads where I rode the R.

Everywhere you look on the R there are lovely touches. I can live without the fake Amal Monoblocs, as much as I can do without black and white TV and travelling on a bus, but I did love the twin digital clocks. These are a loose tribute to the Smith's originals which fell apart on Meriden Bonnies with such enthusiasm, and so are very homely – but they work in a way which Smiths' instruments never did.

The fit and finish of the R is also exemplary. Purists might, and do, say that the R is not a real British bike because it is made in Triumph's Thai factory, but there is no debating the quality control which has produced an outstanding motorcycle.

Is everything perfect in R Land? No, not quite, but it is fixable, at a cost. Unless you are under 25 years of age, the low bars will soon cause agony. Triumph does a higher bar but this is an accessory.

It's the same with a dual seat. Yes, this will fit straight on but it's another cost on top of the already far from cheap £12,000. Finally, the footrests are a long way back – which is fine for the track but not ideal for slow speed riding.

What Triumph needed was a GT version of the R with higher bars, footrests moved forward and, critically, a dual seat. Triumph Italy asked for just such a bike, clearly with memories of the original Ducati Monster in mind, but the management in England didn't agree and so there is no Thruxton GT.

Carol and I were absolutely dead centre, perfect target customers for an R but chose a very low mileage Ducati Sport Classic 1000 GT, which in many ways is a direct competitor for the R – but 10 years older – so Triumph is clearly missing this segment of the market.

Maybe Triumph has a bigger idea in mind because it invested four years' intensive work and about 10 zillion pounds in this project, so I wouldn't be surprised to see the Bonneville family continue to grow during its predicted 10 year life cycle. ■